Ken,

To abundant
success !! ☺

Dustin

R.O.I.
MARKETING
SECRETS
REVEALED

Published by CelebrityPress™, Orlando, FL
A division of The Celebrity Branding Agency®

Celebrity Branding® is a registered trademark
Printed in the United States of America.

ISBN: 978-0-615-38696-6
LCCN: 2010932234

This publication is designed to provide accurate and authoritative information with regard to the subject matter covered. It is sold with the understanding that the publisher is not engaged in rendering legal, accounting, or other professional advice. If legal advice or other expert assistance is required, the services of a competent professional should be sought. The opinions expressed by the authors in this book are not endorsed by CelebrityPress™ and are the sole responsibility of the author rendering the opinion.

Most CelebrityPress™ titles are available at special quantity discounts for bulk purchases for sales promotions, premiums, fundraising, and educational use. Special versions or book excerpts can also be created to fit specific needs.

For more information, please write:

CelebrityPress™,
520 N. Orlando Ave, #44,
Winter Park, FL 32789

or call 1.877.261.4930

Visit us online at **www.CelebrityPressPublishing.com**

R.O.I.
MARKETING
SECRETS
REVEALED

Learn **Million Dollar Secrets** Top Marketers use in
Their Specialty for **Maximum Return On Investment** and
Directly **Increase Your Profits TODAY!**

Table of Contents:

FOREWORD

Marketing for small businesses keeps becoming more and more sophisticated. There are limitless new marketing weapons, tactics, and opportunities. But one thing that has not yet become sophisticated enough for a profit-minded small business is the proper measurement for calculating success.

That measurement is your **return on investment** – your omnipotent ROI. Some businesses simply measure the success of their marketing by sales. But many companies actually lose money while basking in the sham glory of shattered sales records. Some businesses measure marketing success by hits to a website, store traffic, or the conversion rate of visitors to a website becoming paying customers, but those guideposts do not translate into money in your bank account.

The most savvy companies focus on one marketing measurement – profits. But even that stops short because it doesn't factor in the investment that business owners make in their marketing process. And that's precisely why this book has been written – to measure the investment you make in marketing by how much profit is returned to you. More and more, wise company leaders are learning that that's the equation most deserving of your focus.

In the very beginning of marketing, all that mattered was sales. But the very beginning was a long time ago. Today, your ROI is rapidly becoming the gold standard for measuring marketing success. Although many books address themselves to improving your sales – and there's nothing wrong with that – you've got to emphasize your ROI if you want to earn the maximum from your marketing, from your business itself.

Yet, if you bring up ROI in business conversation, the response is usually a blank stare. People can talk themselves 'blue in the face' when discussing their sales or their growth. But when you ask them how they calculate their ROI, you get still another blank stare. Most business owners don't even pay attention to that number.

My own experience has been in helping to create some of the most powerful brands in history: Marlboro, Green Giant, Pillsbury, Sears, Star-Kist Tuna, Oscar Meyer, Mr. Clean, Apple, Hewlett-Packard, Adobe – it's a long list. Every one of those companies had a creative genius contributing to their timeless marketing campaigns. But you can be sure that they also had a financial genius determining their ROI – the single most important number in business.

Those big name companies weren't always big names. They all started as entrepreneurial endeavors. But because they were run by people who understood what marketing is truly all about, they grew and prospered. Whether their marketing budgets were tiny or enormous, they paid close attention to how much it cost them to market, <u>which was their investment in the process</u>, and how much money it returned to them, <u>which was their return</u>. To those business geniuses, their ROI was the name of the game they were playing.

Is it simple to determine your ROI? It is not, because it embraces tracking your marketing and measuring its effectiveness. Because it is so tough to pin down, it is extremely difficult to implement. Richard Seppala, who is famed as the ROI Guy, wrote this book to remove the difficulty for you, simplify the complexity, and help you earn more from your marketing investment than you may have dreamt possible.

I wrote the "Guerrilla Marketing" books to simplify and perfect marketing. Richard has done the same with "ROI Marketing Secrets." This book can put a smile on your face and a pained expression on the face of your clueless competitors.

Jay Conrad Levinson
DeBary, Florida

INTRODUCTION

THE ROI GUY'S GUIDE TO MAXIMIZING PROFITS

Welcome to the first book from *"The ROI Guy,"* (aka Richard Seppala, my not-so-secret identity).

Most of you probably already know what the "ROI" in "ROI Guy" stands for. For those of you who don't - it's not "Really Odd Individual," although I've been accused of being one.

No, "ROI" means "Return on Investment" – getting the most out of what you put into your business. And what this book is all about is making your ROI as high as possible – so your company is making as much money as possible. That's the normal objective of any business, and I'm assuming yours is no different.

In recent years, the economic outlook has been overflowing with bad news. But let's take a 'glass-half-full' approach to looking at today's ROI opportunities – because the overwhelming good news is that there have never been as many cost-effective tools to increase ROI as there are today.

And that's why I've put together this book. I've gathered together some of today's greatest ROI experts to showcase their proven cutting-edge secret methods and services to boost revenues and minimize expenses.

WHAT THIS BOOK WILL REVEAL

You'll be amazed at the ways we've developed, not only to make sure you're getting the most out of your marketing dollars, but that you're also doing everything you can to close sales with customers. Some of these use the newest technology in innovative ways – others are creative variations on tried-and-true but incredibly effective techniques.

All of them, however, can be easily and affordably implemented by your small or medium-sized business. Whether you're a doctor or a lawyer or whether you run a janitorial service, our ROI experts can help you gain more business, make more sales and keep more clients and customers.

These methods are also used extensively by major corporations in their marketing and business systems. Generally, the scale of their operations makes it difficult for the "little guys" – how do you compete with those kinds of multi-million dollar marketing machines? Well, the answer is you *can*. But most small businesspeople don't, because they're either not aware of these tools – or they don't know that they are both available and affordable for them to use.

This book finally puts all these secrets together for the first time – enabling you, if you run your own small or medium-sized business, to 'level the playing

13

field' in a meaningful way.

Now, I realize the vast majority of you have to spend most of your working hours on your core business. That means that, all too often, the critical business elements of marketing, sales and customer service get short shrift - or even ignored - because you simply don't have the time or the staff to deal with it properly. Meanwhile, the bigger companies have entire departments dealing with these crucial areas – and again, you feel like there's no way you can compete.

That's why one of the best things about the ROI methods that our experts and I are about to share with you is the fact that most of them can be implemented with *automated systems.* That means that, once they're put in place, you don't have to waste hours upon hours of valuable time continuing to oversee them. Obviously, you'll want to make adjustments and changes as your business grows and develops, but, in general, you'll find these tools not only cost-effective, but time-efficient.

YOUR OWN ROI PLAN FOR SUCCESS

Most readers would probably think it was enough to have all these awesome ROI secrets revealed and explained to them. But that's not enough for The ROI Guy – because I want to maximize the return on your investment in this book!

To give you more bang for your buck here, and after all our experts have shown you the amazing ways you can grow your profits and lower your costs, we'll walk you through *a complete turnkey ROI plan utilizing all these tools* to show you how they can all work together to create a complete 'full circle' marketing plan with impact to spare.

You'll see how using these techniques across a wide variety of media – everything from direct mail to social media – can build your brand and sell your services in exciting new ways… ways that reinforce each other and keep you 'top-of-mind' with your customers.

You don't have to use all these techniques – depending on your business and your customer base, some of them will work better than others. But how will you know which ones are most effective? Well, I'll also show you how to *measure your ROI* for each separate campaign – giving you a foolproof, completely scientific way to know what to concentrate on, in your marketing efforts.

HOW I BECAME THE ROI GUY

Before we get into the book, I'd also like to tell you a little bit about how I became "The ROI Guy."

If you've ever watched the Oscars, the Emmys, or any of the other ten million awards shows on television, you'll undoubtedly remember many winners at the podium - after thanking their religion, their manager, their agent and their Botox provider – saying they wouldn't be there without their spouse.

With me, that's literally true.

I got into the ROI measurement business because my wife is a dentist. She was frustrated because she was spending a lot of money on advertising – and didn't think she was getting anything out of it. As I really hate having a frustrated wife, I decided to put her efforts to the test – and I implemented a system designed to see if her marketing was a waste of money, or worth the expense.

It turned out her basic advertising messages were effective – but one big problem was that some ad placements worked a whole lot better than others. And the other big problem was that, when leads were generated by the ads, her staff wasn't handling the phone calls coming in correctly (that's not a unique case, by the way – incoming calls from interested customers are frequently mishandled and cause a lot of potential new revenue to just fall through the cracks).

She learned that it wasn't enough to create great marketing. That marketing also had to be put in front of the right people, at the right place, at the right time – and the people it did reach had to be handled correctly when they called to inquire further about using her services. Yes, it's hard to believe that you can 'blow' a call from an interested potential customer – but it happens more often than not!

Just making the needed adjustments to both her marketing campaign and how her staff dealt with phone calls did amazing things – mostly by sending her profits through the roof. And that made me think, if it worked that well for my wife, it's going to work that well for other people – even ones that I'm not married to.

Today, I have a wide variety of clients in a wide variety of businesses; you'll hear from one of them in a later chapter. And, in continuing to expand my expertise and range of services, I also interact and work with a number of other ROI experts, who you'll also be hearing from throughout this book. *We all have made it our life's work to help small businesses save time and money – and increase revenues at the same time.* That's what ROI is all about.

So enjoy the book – and please, take advantage of our knowledge and experience to help your business become an **ROI superstar**!

CHAPTER 1
THE FOUR PILLARS OF ROI

by Richard Seppala, The ROI Guy

Before we get into what our experts have to share about their secret methods on how to boost your marketing ROI, I want to spend this chapter just talking about the whole concept of ROI.

I mean, it's simple, right? ROI. Return On Investment. You put money into something, you expect to get something back.

Well, I have to tell you that it's actually not that simple. Because you don't simply invest money in building your business. Let's face it, if you're running your own small or medium-sized business, you're investing almost all of *yourself* in that business. The business becomes an extension of you – and for everything you put into it, you quite rightly expect to get something back.

That's where ROI comes in.

Because it doesn't matter if you're working 24/7 to make your business a success, if you're not working towards the right goals and/or if you're ignoring crucial aspects of your business. It doesn't even matter if you're the best you can be at your core business, if other factors you've put in place around your expertise are shooting you down on a daily basis.

Example – you're an optometrist. You've bought the most cutting-edge hi-tech equipment to deliver the best and most comprehensive eye exams in your area. Awesome – you're going to own the market, right?

Well, you might – except you've hired a receptionist with the personality of a lump of coal, you're charging three times as much for an eye exam as anyone else and you're ignoring the real profit center of your business, selling fashionable eyeglass frames.

In other words, you'll probably end up selling all that fancy equipment on eBay.

Don't get me wrong – you should be the best you can be at what you do. It does matter. *But it's very far from the only thing that matters.*

Anyone who remembers the Betamax vs. VHS videotape war in the early days of home video systems can attest to that. Even though most professionals rated the Betamax system as better quality, VHS won the marketing war and came out on top. Then there's Coke and Pepsi – most consumers, in blind taste tests, actually prefer Pepsi. Coke's superior marketing, however, puts it over the top in sales.

The most potent business combination is a winning product or service combined with smart marketing that's ROI tested and proven. It's a delicate balance – but it can be done more easily than you think, using the tools we'll be detailing in chapters to come.In this chapter, however, we're going to look at what I call the four pillars of ROI – the four most important things I believe every business owner invests on a daily basis and deserves a return on, if everything is handled properly. None of these pillars are things you want to see go to waste.

ROI PILLAR #1: MONEY

As I said at the beginning of this chapter, money is the most obvious thing you invest in your business. At least it's the most obvious thing when you look at your P&L sheet!

Some people think that the more money they spend, the more they'll get back - the old "it takes money to make money" school of thought. There's no question having a lot of money available opens up a lot of options. But it's also true that you don't necessarily solve a problem by throwing money at it.

For example, say you've decided it's time to put *your* money where your mouth is. So you're going to invest ten thousand dollars in a big new marketing campaign for your company. You pick your favorite radio station – you like it, so other people must, right? – and you blow your whole budget on continually running commercials for your business on it.

Well, it could turn out that the bulk of your customers don't listen to that radio station. And maybe the radio commercial you produced was confusing and nobody quite understood your marketing message. You ended up generating twenty leads out of the campaign – which means you spent $500 a head and you *know* you won't make that much back from each of those twenty people. Especially since the majority of them made one inquiry call and you never heard from them again. Oh, and you can't get in touch with them – your receptionist forgot to get their contact details.

The point is it doesn't matter how much money you spend, if you don't spend it smart!

You need to test the various advertising venues and messages to see which is most effective for your target market. That ten thousand you poured into radio you might have been able to avoid spending altogether by doing some social media or other online marketing.

…And you also need to equip your business to properly handle the leads you *do* generate, or it doesn't even matter how effective your marketing was!

When I work with my clients, I scientifically measure the ROI of each individual advertisement or marketing placement to see how many leads each one is generating and how effective that advertisement is. And we discuss how incoming sales calls are handled – and how that system can be improved. I'll talk more about that in the next chapter.

ROI PILLAR #2: TIME

Every small business owner finds his biggest nemesis is often the clock. There are only so many hours in the day – and only so many tasks you can really get done at an optimal level.

Making that problem even worse is that often you're the only one who sees the "Big Picture" of your business – so you're reluctant to delegate too much to employees who don't have the experience or expertise to follow through on jobs critical to your business.

That means your time can be as precious an investment as money when it comes to your ROI – and you don't want to waste it on projects that don't pay off.

When an owner is overextended, that means something has to suffer – and much of the time it's marketing that takes the fall. If you're a service provider, such as a chiropractor or dentist, it's hard to concentrate on how best to sell your services after cracking five backs back into shape or performing three back-to-back root canals. Also, marketing isn't usually what you majored in at school, and you may not feel confident in that area.

So you end up *reacting* instead of acting – and wasting more time than you would if you had structured, automatic marketing systems in place. That means you could find yourself putting together a perfunctory, ineffective ad for a re-served placement at the last minute – trying to follow up with new customer inquiries between appointments when your concentration is scattered - compiling a marketing database from 20 email lists which may have duplications or obsolete information – or desperately trying to pull off a new marketing campaign too quickly because you just noticed your new business numbers are 'falling off a cliff', because you haven't done any outside marketing at all for months.

"Last-minute marketing" is only a good idea when you're taking advantage of a topical situation or special event, not as a way of life. You'll find yourself dealing with marketing in a much more orderly, easier and impactful way if you put the right ROI systems to work for your business – because that means you can spend less time on marketing and get more results. A true ROI achievement!

ROI PILLAR #3: IMAGE

This one might sound strange to the average business owner – you might ask yourself, "How am I investing my image in something? And how could that be a bad thing?"

Well, assuming that you've run your business to establish yourself as professional, trustworthy and reliable as possible, it could be a very bad thing – because all of those valuable attributes are tied up in your image. And you've spent many years investing your own credibility into that image. It's one of your most crucial intangible assets – and something that you've worked hard to build up so you could get a good return on it, in terms of having a good reputation and word-of-mouth that attracts new business.

But just as it takes a long time to create a positive image with the public, it also takes a very short time to tear it down. You can probably think of countless entertainers and politicians that have been instantly destroyed by a scandal that grabbed all the headlines for a news cycle. And you probably also remember how long those 'celebs' and prominent people spent building their successful images, only to have them wrecked in a matter of moments.

Every day, in every interaction your business has with a potential or exist-ing customer, it's your image on the line – even though it may be one of your staff that may be representing you, or perhaps even merely one of your market-ing pieces.

Any time you put something out in the name of you or your business, you're risking tarnishing that image. It could be something silly like a misspelling in the subject line of a mass email – or something more serious like your employee inappropriately losing their temper with one of your clients. Whatever it is, it reflects on you and your business as a whole.

Again, when you're not paying attention to the details that can affect peo-ple's perception of you and your business, you risk lowering your image ROI. What you want to happen is for your image to automatically work *for* you, not against you. There are many ROI methods and tools that allow you to not only safeguard your image, but also to *control* it to send out the message about your business you want sent out.

Image can be a powerful positive for you – if used correctly. And we'll have some ways for you to do just that in the chapters to come.

ROI PILLAR #4: STAFF

Your employees can be "The Perfect Storm" when it comes to creating a disastrous ROI – because you put your time, money *and* image – all three of the previous pillars - into the people you hire to work at your business. Think about everything you invest in them - you have to spend time training them, you have to pay them, and you have to make them aware of the objectives of your busi-ness. It's a *huge* investment.

And a critical one, especially when it comes to the staff that regularly in-teracts with potential and existing customers. You absolutely need a high ROI from those particular employees. If they're not treating your customers right – or if they have no training in how to sell your services in the most pro-active way – they're actively *damaging* your business on a day-to-day business.

Conversely, someone with the right training and the right personality will build your business to an incredible level without you even being aware of how much they're contributing.

You can spend all the money in the world on a marketing campaign to generate leads – and it's the same as 'flushing it down the toilet' if, when that campaign actually persuades someone to call your business, the person you have answering the phone treats the person with indifference or disdain.

This is why, with my clients, I make it a point of advising them how to best train employees to help maximize your ROI across the board. We'll talk more about that in the next chapter.

As you can hopefully see, achieving a meaningful ROI is more than just comparing how much money you spent on marketing against how much you made from it. It's looking closely at all the processes along the way: from what message you put out there, …where you place that message, …how you place it, …how generated leads are handled, …and how you do your follow-up marketing.

But enough about the problems of obtaining a great ROI – it's time to start moving on to some amazing and awesome solutions. In the next chapter, I'll share some of my exclusive "ROI Guy" secrets – and show you how I solve many of these issues for my clients with simple, easy-to-use systems and tools!

ABOUT RICHARD

Your ROI Guy – Richard Seppala

Richard Seppala, a.k.a. Your ROI Guy, has spent years in direct sales and marketing and is now using his knowledge to help businesses across the nation. He has been referred to as the Call Tracking Expert, and has been featured on CBS, ABC, NBC and FOX, as well is in The Wall Street Journal. As the president of Total Census Solutions, Richard uses his extensive experience to help his clients with one of their biggest marketing dilemmas – knowing their marketing ROI.

How did Richard obtain such a deep understanding of ROI when it comes to marketing campaigns? He spent more than a decade as the vice president of sales and marketing for top providers within the long-term care industry. During that time, he developed unique and creative marketing programs that consistently surpassed census goals and financial satisfaction. He learned early on that the key to marketing success is knowing your numbers.

Richard now provides innovative programs and technologies to other businesses, to allow them to easily monitor, track and quantify the effectiveness of their marketing campaigns. He has also created systems that help companies improve upon their customer service and in-office presentations.

If you are ready to market with confidence, contact Your ROI Guy today!

CHAPTER 2
HOW THE ROI GUY RAISES YOUR ROI

by Richard Seppala, The ROI Guy

As I mentioned in the first chapter, when it comes to marketing, a lot of small and medium-sized business people aren't really sure what works – or how to figure out what works. It can feel like trying to hold target practice in the dark. Again, it's not their main business or specialty, it's just something *they know they have to do.*

Kind of like how your parents made you 'eat your veggies' as a kid.

Because business owners know they have to do it – or they won't develop new customers and clients - they kind of shrug their shoulders, grit their teeth and do their best. And, unfortunately, many of them end up wasting a lot more money than they should on marketing that has little to no chance of working.

As *The ROI Guy*, that just sends shivers down my spine. *It doesn't have to be like that.* Which is why I continue to develop and implement easy, affordable systems that take the guesswork out of my clients' marketing and sales efforts.

My fivefold mission is to:

1. Make sure their marketing message works
2. Evaluate which marketing placements are most effective
3. Track incoming sales calls and capture lead information
4. Ensure that new potential customer calls are handled correctly
5. Help convert those incoming calls to actual sales

By providing a comprehensive start-to-finish approach to their marketing, I can give them an exact reading on the ROI of each campaign or placement. I can help make sure, at each step of the process, that they're doing everything they possibly can to generate new leads and close sales with those leads.

TRACKING YOUR MARKETING

That process begins right when you do your actual marketing. Whether you're doing direct mail, online ads, print ads, outdoor or whatever, I can immediately find out which venue as well as which message is generating the most leads for you.

How do I do that? I assign each individual marketing piece or advertisement its own toll-free phone number. In other words, your direct mail would have one phone number for an interested customer to call – and your print ad would offer a different one.

Now, all these phone numbers are actually internet VoIP (Voice over Internet Protocol) numbers – anyone who calls them automatically gets forwarded to a single line at your business (whichever number you specify), but, as the call is going through, my system captures that call as well as the caller ID information and automatically tallies it online.

That means I will be able to pinpoint automatically *exactly how many calls each individual ad generated.* You'll know instantly which of your marketing placements brings you the best ROI – and which consistently underperform. That means you can spend those marketing dollars much more wisely – concentrating on the sectors where you can be sure of a higher ROI and laying off the sectors that just don't deliver.

And wouldn't that be awesome for your business? After all, I'm sure, whatever your business is, you're expected to achieve some measurable results. Marketing should be no different.

Usually you have to pay a high premium to get your advertising message to the most people. But often, it's not important to reach the most people – it's more important to reach the *right* people. It doesn't matter if your message is delivered to millions – if your target market isn't in that group. For instance, selling ballet lessons in the middle of a football game would cost you a fortune and probably not get you a lot of students. Then again, who knows? Maybe it would!

My system is the way to find out. It shows you point blank what works and what doesn't. And the money you'll save in marketing by having that knowledge will add up to a whole lot more than you pay to use that system, trust me.

MEASURING YOUR MESSAGE

Another way I use the individual phone numbers I assign to separate campaigns is to see which marketing message attracts the most business for you.

Since my wife is a dentist, let's use her practice for an example. Maybe she's not sure what will attract more new patients - advertising her new teeth whitening process or promoting the fact that she caters to "dental chickens."

My system makes this incredibly easy to track. By placing two sets of ads – one pushing the whitening scheme, the other focusing on painless dentistry

– with two different phone numbers, we can easily see which ad generates the most leads – by seeing which one prompts the most phone calls.

Again, this is incredibly valuable information to have. If you know what will motivate potential new customers to call you, that's pure gold. My system also gives you an advantage in terms of knowing ahead of time what service a lead is calling about. But we'll talk about that a little later.

HOW *NOT* TO HANDLE AN INCOMING SALES CALL

Yes, my system's great at tracking what advertising works. And also help-ing you make sure that you're getting incoming calls from potential customers as a result of your marketing efforts. But all effort is for nothing if those phone calls are completely mishandled.

You could have the best marketing and advertising campaign in the world driving people to call you *immediately* – a campaign with a potentially amazing ROI – but if you lose your generated leads at the point of sale, that money all gets flushed down the drain.

For instance, maybe you've got a receptionist prone to going outside for a cigarette and forgetting to turn on the voice mail system.

A prospect calls because of a great direct mail piece you sent out. They're ready to do business. But, instead of getting a person answering their call, or, at least, a message, all they get is…, "Ring. Ring. Ring. Ring. Ring."

I could type out ten more "Ring's," but you get the idea. You're not making that sale. Probably ever.

Now let's go with an alternate scenario. Perhaps, as luck would have it, the generated lead calls *after* your receptionist's smoke break. The receptionist says, in a tired voice, "Hi, so-and-so's office, can I help you?"

"Yes," the prospect says, "I'm really interested in so-and-so's so and so."

"Oh," says the Receptionist. "Okay. That costs so-and so."

"Oh…thanks. 'Bye."

Dial tone. The receptionist shrugs and looks forward to another cigarette break. No skin off their teeth. The prospect who hung up? They haven't lost anything either. They'll just go on with their lives.

Meanwhile, here's what *you've* lost. A sale. More potential future business. Contact information. And a big dent in your overall ROI.

HOW *TO* HANDLE AN INCOMING SALES CALL

That receptionist, instead of just giving the cost, or answering any perfunc-tory question with a "yes" or "no", should have instead engaged the potential customer on a human, personal level.

Examples: "Why are you interested in the service? Well, here's what the service can do for you. Other customers say it's done this or that for them. What else can I tell you? Would you like to come in for a free consultation?" Those are just a few things that receptionist could have said to keep that person on the line and make them feel more comfortable about using your product or service.

That's why I also advocate recording the calls of whoever answers your phones (even if it's you). The purpose is not to spy on employees or to catch them on personal calls – it's merely to see how incoming sales calls can be handled better and how the process can be improved. In other words, we make it a positive coaching experience, not a negative calling-on-the-carpet kind of session.

Over two-thirds of incoming calls are routinely mishandled, according to studies. There's an art to converting a caller with a question to a sale. And we know how to train people in that art.

Again, you've invested a lot in your employees and you should expect a high ROI. This is one way to get it.

A WHISPER TO THE WISE

Listen closely – because a little whisper can mean a big difference to your bottom line.

As I already mentioned, using separate phone lines for different marketing messages means I can measure which message is working better.

What I didn't mention is that this can also deliver a big advantage to who-ever's answering your phones – thanks to our "whisper feature," which tells your staff what people are calling about *before* you talk to them!

Let's go back to our example of the dentist selling a new teeth whitening procedure. When a generated lead calls the phone number on that advertise-ment, just before that call is put through to the staff person on your end, a "whis-per" will come over the phone saying *"Teeth Whitening lead."* Or whatever you want the whisper to say.

That way, your staff will instantly *know* why this person is calling and can shift into "sales" mode. They can get their game on, maybe pull out the teeth whitening info if they need to, and be instantly ready to sell your service. And if it turns out that whoever is answering the phone at that moment isn't the right person to sell the teeth whitening service, they can immediately transfer the call to the right person.

'Forewarned is forearmed' as they say – and it's a lot easier to get a sales call off on the right foot when you know (a) it *is* a sales call and (b) what spe-cific product or service that the person is calling about.

BRIDGING THE HUMAN FACTOR

There's another system I offer to my clients that bypasses the unpredictable "human factor" altogether when it comes to incoming sales calls. I call it "The ROI Bridge." "The Bridge" accomplishes everything you want to accomplish with an incoming sales call – and it does it *automatically* without you having to lift a finger – or worry about who's available to answer the phone.

Bear with me – we're going to use the teeth whitening procedure again. I can't help it, I just love white teeth – maybe that's why I married a dentist!

Let's say a person sees our ad for the teeth whitening and calls the number we've placed on it. A recorded message offers to send that person free information on the new procedure and the dental practice itself (an all-important "Call to Action") if they leave their contact information.

With "The Bridge" software package, we then record their information and message if there is one, and automatically transcribe and upload their contact info into the business's CRM (Customer Relationship Management) software.

What advantages does this give a business? Well, (a) a staff member can call the prospect back when they have the time to conduct a productive conversation, (b) they'll also be prepared to sell the specific service the prospect is calling about, (c) the prospect's contact information is digitally stored and can be automatically used in the next marketing campaign, and (d) you don't lose track of a potential new client or customer since everything has been recorded.

Most importantly, you're not at the mercy of having to deal with the call when your office might be at its busiest. You need time and space to really manage sales calls effectively. Automating everything puts those sales calls on your timetable – and, as we've already noted, when you run a small or medium-sized business, time can be more valuable than money!

Not only that, you can cut down or even eliminate staff positions because an all-in-one ROI process like this means you don't need to have people 'inputting' contact info or handling sales calls all day. It all gets done for one low affordable monthly charge.

I've worked hard – and continue to work hard – to optimize every step of the marketing process so that it works as well as possible for your business - and your ROI is as high as can be.

Marketing doesn't have to be like holding target practice in the dark. You can know how to hit the bulls-eye every time by using simple, affordable systems that guarantee you results. And that's what *The ROI Guy* is all about!

In the next chapter, one of my clients will tell you how my systems and secrets work for him to help deliver the best possible ROI to his company.

ABOUT RICHARD

Your ROI Guy – Richard Seppala

Richard Seppala, a.k.a. Your ROI Guy, has spent years in direct sales and marketing and is now using his knowledge to help businesses across the nation. He has been referred to as the Call Tracking Expert, and has been featured on CBS, ABC, NBC and FOX, as well is in The Wall Street Journal. As the president of Total Census Solutions, Richard uses his extensive experience to help his clients with one of their biggest marketing dilemmas – knowing their marketing ROI.

How did Richard obtain such a deep understanding of ROI when it comes to marketing campaigns? He spent more than a decade as the vice president of sales and marketing for top providers within the long-term care industry. During that time, he developed unique and creative marketing programs that consistently surpassed census goals and financial satisfaction. He learned early on that the key to marketing success is knowing your numbers.

Richard now provides innovative programs and technologies to other businesses, to allow them to easily monitor, track and quantify the effectiveness of their marketing campaigns. He has also created systems that help companies improve upon their customer service and in-office presentations.

If you are ready to market with confidence, contact Your ROI Guy today!

CHAPTER 3
ROI GUY CASE STUDY: "YOU'RE DUMB IF YOU DON'T DO IT"

by Dr. Scott Schumann

Yes, you read that chapter title correctly – "You're Dumb If You Don't Do It." That's basically what I tell everyone when they ask if they should try some of Richard "The ROI Guy" Seppala's amazing hi-tech marketing measurement techniques.

I say, "You're dumb if you don't do it," because *there's no reason not to do it*. His services are really affordable and, between the money you'll save on marketing and the increase in revenues you'll realize, you'll see an almost-immediate and positive impact on your bottom line.

I'm already estimating he's going to save me $20,000 to $30,000 in marketing costs next year – and I can't even begin to describe how much he's increased my profits just through using his new patient marketing and conversion services.

What I really like about Richard – besides the wonderful fact that he saves and makes me money - is that he provides me with all the latest and incredibly effective ROI tools that he develops.

I like to use the newest cutting-edge equipment in my dentistry practice at Grove City Dental near Columbus, Ohio – it does more for my patients. And I think Richard's systems also do more for his clients. You don't get vague "well, maybe try this or maybe try that" stabs in the dark like other marketing gurus sometimes give you.

Richard provides real, concrete results that enable businesses like mine to make smart and informed marketing choices. You can actually see what you're doing wrong – and right, for that matter – and act on that information.

Not only that, but Richard helps keep my staff operating at the highest level possible. He allows all of us – yes, even me – to see where we could be going wrong with patient interactions that might cost us a lot of business in the long-run. If you're open to what he and his partners have to tell you, you're pretty much guaranteed to succeed.

THE ROI GUY AND ME

I met Richard around two years ago. His wife, Lisa, is also a dentist with a practice similar to mine and we often compare notes. In 2007, at a dental conference, Richard was there and we ended up hanging out in the back and talking (we were supposed to be listening to the speaker…so I guess our ROI as far as he was concerned wasn't as high as it should have been!).

Up until then, I did pretty much the traditional marketing stuff most dentists do. Business cards, giving out toothbrushes with our name and number, the Yellow Pages. A little internet, but not much.

Richard changed all that.

When he began talking about using different phone numbers to track various marketing placements, I was amazed – I had never heard anything like this before. And what you need to know about me is that I fought hard to get a great easy-to-remember phone number for Grove City Dental: 801-1000. I was in love with that number and really proud that I managed to get it. So while the tracking number concept seemed exciting, it was hard to let go of good ol' 801-1000.

But I did let go – and once I began seeing the results, I suddenly didn't care if my once-beloved phone number disappeared altogether.

Richard also started me on using Infusion CRM (Customer Relationship Management) software in conjunction with his "Bridge" package. Thanks to that, incoming sales calls to the tracking numbers he's assigned our business are automatically recorded and the caller's name and address are input into the software database, so we can instantly market to them again later with a follow-up campaign.

This was a godsend. Yes, my staff used to tell me they were already manually collecting all this data when they answered phone calls. But when Richard began monitoring the calls, he told me that this just wasn't the case. Nothing against my staff – after all, they won "Best Team" in a nationwide contest held by Ed O'Keefe's Dentist Profits organization earlier this year, so I certainly know they're top-notch. It's just a human thing – and, as I'm quick to admit, I was as guilty as anyone for not writing down important contact information from a caller interested in our services.

Now, nothing slips through the cracks, thanks to Richard's "Bridge" system. Not only that, we can access those recorded incoming sales calls through Richard's website and go over what we did right and what we did wrong. With that kind of instant review, my staff actually enjoys taking a listen and pointing out their own mistakes. As long as it's a positive learning experience, nobody takes it personally.

One new service we just started using from Richard is the Video Mystery Patient, which he talks about in another chapter in this book. Basically, what happens is someone calls pretending to be a new patient and books an appointment with us. That person comes in, armed with a tiny video camera on their person, and secretly tapes the entire experience – from the greeting by my receptionist to my interaction with them.

And this is where I was proudest of our operation at my practice.

When the "mystery patient" arrived, after making an appointment in advance, we had no idea he was the plant. He ended up actually paying for treatment from us – and he's now one of our regular patients – even though he lives about an hour away from our offices. That's right – *we converted the guy who was supposed to test how good our conversion was.* Doesn't get much better than that.

THE JOY OF TRACKING NUMBERS

As I mentioned earlier, I was reluctant to give up the phone number I had already marketed as much as humanly possible. But now, thanks to Richard, I've got between 20 and 30 different tracking numbers in use with different marketing placements, including:

- Online Yellow Pages
- Traditional Yellow Pages
- Local sports team and cheerleading team sponsorships
- PPC Google advertising
- Different mini-websites
- Local Cable TV advertising
- Online video advertising
- Cell phone texts to patients
- Email blasts
- Newsletters
- ValPak
- And more…

We've put tracking numbers on folding chairs we donated to an Ohio State football tailgate party - we even made one of our staff's cell phone number our tracking number one weekend for a special campaign, so she could book appointments remotely when the office was closed!

So, yes, we have a lot of fun using the tracking numbers in every conceivable way.

And when I say every conceivable way…

Well, I golf. I'm not a patient golfer – I just like to hit the ball and, as I like to say, learn to not suck as much at it. So when I lose a ball by hitting it into the rough – I don't go looking for it. I just get out a new ball and continue on with my game.

Which made me think…well, I should get *something* out of all those balls I lose. After all, other people find them, I'm sure, and get a great freebee.

So I decided to put the Grove City Dental logo on the balls I use…along, of course, with one of Richard's magic tracking numbers. And the best part is… yes, we actually got some calls from my lost golf balls!

Incidentally, I also put our logo on golf tees too…but the tees were too small to fit a tracking number on. You do what you can.

On the serious side, Richard has also been invaluable in helping me market to more niche target groups. I've got enough family dentistry patients – those pretty much come in on their own at this point as I have a well-established practice in the area. Now I'm interested in increasing profitability with more implant and sedation dentistry patients, as well as more pre-qualified credit patients.

With Richard's tracking numbers I can quickly find out which campaign is working with these kind of potential clients – and which one isn't. I can test which headline works on an internet or print ad – and which one doesn't. I can even try out different online videos with different tracking numbers. It's all valuable research and the numbers come in instantly with the generated calls. Best of all, according to my staff anyway, all the contact information from these generated calls, as I said earlier, gets automatically loaded into the Infusion software.

I really look at The ROI Guy as an incredible resource and a real marketing partner. Whenever I need a new tracking number for a new placement, I just have to pick up the phone and he's there with one. He's helped me and my staff become as good as we can possibly get at marketing and customer service - and it has paid off in so many ways, I've lost count.

As I said at the beginning, he's also helped me thin out the marketing that just wasn't effective. There were placements and campaigns I thought were really good and were working. Turns out they weren't. With Richard's hard numbers, I quickly discovered what I could easily get rid of:- ads I thought were great that generated nothing, websites that I thought were converting but weren't, and other marketing that just simply wasn't worth the money.

What's fun and exciting is that he's also open to developing new processes and systems with me. Right now, we're working on a way to accurately measure patient conversion, from their first sign of interest all the way through their first office visit.

So, yes, I've gotten a great ROI from The ROI Guy. Now, you may be wondering, "Should I try out his services?"

Well, if you read the title of the chapter, you already know my answer.
SCOTT SCHUMANN.

ABOUT SCOTT

Dr. Scott Schumann, a native of Columbus, Ohio, grew up loving the Buckeyes, playing sports, and collecting rocks. Dr. Schumann and his wife Robin live in downtown Columbus with their dog, Bourbon, the boxer. Dr. Schumann loves supporting the local arts, sponsoring little league teams, golfing, fishing and attending concerts as well as NAS-CAR events.

Dr. Schumann graduated from Ohio State University Dental School in 1989 and then completed his residency training at University of Texas Health Science Center at San Antonio in 1991, with training and certification in advanced dental techniques, dental implants and sedation dentistry. He also received a fellowship in Hospital Dentistry, helping him to excel in assisting his medically compromised patients. After returning to Columbus Ohio, Dr. Schumann started his career and began teaching in the Advanced Dentistry Clinic at the Ohio State University, teaching dental residents advanced cosmetic, implant, hospital, and sedation dentistry for ten years.

An active member in the Columbus Dental Society, Ohio Dental Association, American Dental Association, Academy of General Dentists, American Academy of Cosmetic Dentists and the American Dental Society of Anesthesiology, Dr. Schumann and his team have kept up to date on the latest developments in dentistry.

Dr. Scott Schumann's office in Grove City, a suburb 8 minutes south of downtown Columbus, Ohio, is often referred to by clients as "fun" and "cool"—2 words not often associated with dentistry. Dr. Schumann and his staff are well known for their love of helping their patients achieve the smile they always dreamed of and now through his innovative systems, Dr. Schuman is helping dentists around the country achieve the lifestyle and success they always dreamed of while helping patients change their lives. His professional team and his facility, with amazing new technological advancements, makes each patient visit as fun as possible without guilt or embarrassment while allowing him to leverage his time and experience to grow his dental practice.

Dr. Scott Schumann has been published in multiple research journals, as well as featured in *21 Principles of Smile Design* and *Shift Happens*. He has presented at various conferences and events and has been quoted in the Wall Street Journal, USA Today, and Newsweek and well as appeared on America's PremierExperts® TV show on NBC, CBS, ABC and FOX.

To learn more about Dr. Schumann and how he helps to grow dental practices visit www.dentalofficesystemsmadeeasy.com

Or call toll-free 888-496-1250

CHAPTER 4
STOP THE HIRING INSANITY

by Jay Henderson, CEO, Real Talent Hiring

I f you own a business, finding great people to work for your company is one of the most important things you do - and one of the most difficult.

All you need is 'a crystal ball' - or some serious luck!

More often than not – hiring is trial and error. And I don't have to tell you, the error part gets really expensive. Hire too many of the wrong people and it can bring your company down.

Typically, you go through resumes, pick a few you like – interview them (hopefully more than once) and check references. You might even hire someone as a favor to a friend. And you might get feedback from key people on your staff, but eventually – because the buck stops with you – you have to 'roll the dice'. Then you pray.

All too often, you spend thousands of dollars to do this dance, only to discover it's not working out. Little by little, you discover your new hire is not really who you thought they were at all - so you try to save them. Most of the time, you can't make it work - so eventually you have to sever the relationship and start over.

How could they have looked so good? How could you have been so easily fooled? How were they able to 'fake you out'?

If you had only known.

You're not alone - because in today's world, there are 'how-to-interview' coaches, professional resume-writers, interview courses and other "tricks of the trade" turning out armies of perfectly polished 'time bombs' that look better than they are. What I mean is… some people are really good at getting jobs - just not very good at doing them.

It's what I like to call "interview misdirection" – and its costing companies like yours millions of dollars every year.

Would you be shocked to learn the majority of resumes – not just a few - but *the majority* – <u>contain false information</u>? I didn't think so.

And the interview? When people are coached on exactly what to say and how to dance around less than flattering issues – you're just not getting a true picture.

And did you ever check with a former boss on what they think? Surely they will 'shoot straight' with you about what your potential hire is really like, right? "Wrong!" Our lawsuit-happy culture makes it risky for them 'to spill the beans' on a former employee – even one they may have just fired. Your "perfect" candidate could have been caught stealing them blind and they still may not tell you.

The point is, the traditional hiring system is far from perfect. So how can you make great decisions and hire great people?

Maybe I can help…

My name is Jay Henderson – and my specialty is getting 'inside the heads' of your potential hires to uncover their very real biases, their strengths, their weakness, and the things they're not telling you – *before* you hire them.

With my totally unique, scientifically-based system, you'll never be fooled again. There is no way for your job candidate to "game" the system… I guarantee it.

It's working right now for America's best companies. You can visit my website at www.RealTalentHiring.com for an impressive list of our clients. They range from small businesses with only a handful of employees – to companies in the *Fortune 500,* … even the New York Yankees.

THE METHOD BEHIND THE MAGIC

The system I use was designed by a renowned philosopher and economist whose groundbreaking research was nominated for a Nobel Prize in 1973. Still the only system of it's kind in the world, he was first to discover a method for accurately measuring these two critical factors… how people *think* and how they *make decisions*. It's a very different approach from the typical behavior profile.

Just imagine how valuable it would be if you could predict your potential hire's success based on your knowledge of how they think and make decisions.

If our biases, the way we think and make decisions, changed from day to day - it would be pretty tough. But the good news is, they rarely, if ever, change. That makes all of us more predictable than we would have ever imagined.

What if you had a crystal clear picture of a person's biases *before* you hired them? You could eliminate the risk of having to spend weeks or months observing their performance. You can predict their performance.

I know firsthand, because it worked on me.

MY LUCKY DAY

A few years ago, I applied for a job with a company that uses the principles of sports psychology to coach people to higher levels of performance. I had what turned out to be one of the most important job interviews of my life.

Before the interview, they had given me a simple 36 item exercise to complete. I couldn't imagine what they could possibly learn about me from this process but I followed instructions and completed the exercise in less than 20 minutes. I had filled out typical profiles before – but believe me, this was nothing like anything I had ever seen – there weren't even any questions.

During the interview I was asked the most pointed, in-my-world question anyone had ever asked me. This man knew things about me no one could have or should have known. I sat there stunned. How could he possibly know this?

Fortunately, what they saw in my response to the 36 item list was good for me – I got the job – and before long…

I LEARNED THE SECRET

I've been passionate about how the mind works since I was a kid. I always wanted to understand why some people always seem to win and some always seem to struggle.

Looking back on it, I got really lucky when I was just 19. My dad gave me the audio program of Stephen R. Covey's now-famous "Seven Habits of Highly Effective People." That was before the book was released and before Stephen became a worldwide consulting star.

Something in Covey's message really rang true with me. I listened to those tapes until I could almost recite them from memory. When the book came out a few years later, I read it over and over as well.

I was hooked – so right then and there, I set a goal to work for Stephen Covey.

It wasn't going to be easy. Covey's organization was based in Utah – I was living in North Carolina. I was young, and had no experience in the training industry. But as you know, when goals are strong enough – answers come – and that's what happened for me. I would go to school in Utah and that would put me closer to the Covey group.

SERENDIPTY

I remember it like it was yesterday. I woke up one beautiful North Carolina morning – packed my car – and drove across the country to Utah. I didn't have a place to stay, and I didn't have a job – but I knew what I wanted. So I just did it.

About three months after I arrived in Provo, I was driving past a building I knew was part of the Covey Leadership Center. I had a clear overpowering desire to pull over. So that's exactly what I did.

I walked in the front door, and this lady was standing there. She asked "Can I help you?" And for some reason, I answered, "I'm here to interview for a position." She asked if I'd seen the ad.

I said, "No, I hadn't seen the ad." I didn't even know they were interviewing. I was just following my impression. But for some reason – maybe they could see my passion – they interviewed and hired me right there on the spot.

Over the next five great years, I learned 'a ton' from Stephen and his group – and I fell in love with an industry I have worked in for the past 20 years.

My experiences at Covey were great – but I decided to move to another Utah company which led me to an opportunity to learn from another true genius, Wayne Carpenter. Wayne is the guru who refined, redesigned and computerized the system we use today in companies of all sizes all across America.

I have had the good fortune to be personally trained and to study under Wayne for the past 15 years – and today, I am one of only eight people in the world to be Master Certified by him to do what I do… help people like you make the best possible hiring decisions.

THE SECRET HIRING WEAPON

The process we use for hiring just the right person is amazingly simple but don't be fooled – it's amazingly accurate. I like to think of it as an MRI for hiring.

Once you decide you're interested in a candidate, I get involved in the process to help you decide if this job candidate is the right fit for your business. And it's 'oh so easy'. Your job candidate goes online and completes a simple 36 item exercise. It takes less than 20 minutes.

When we have the results, you'll get a comprehensive 4-page report. At a glance – you'll know how your candidate *thinks* and *makes decisions*. You'll know your level of risks in hiring this person and so much more.

My job is to tell you things about your job candidate you could never discover any other way. …Not through a resume, an interview, a former boss, or from any of the most popular profiles being used in today's marketplace.

Our system takes the profile process to levels that are 'way' beyond behavior and personality. You'll know more than you could have ever imagined about their competencies and skills. You'll immediately see your job candidate's strengths - including what motivates them, their weaknesses, even the quality of their day-to-day decisions, and the areas in which they need to grow.

You'll know whether or not they CAN do the job. You'll know if they WILL do the job. And you'll know if they can get the job done in your company and perform in the specific role you're hiring them for. Again, you'll know how they think and make a decision - which makes their potential performance highly predictable.

You will no longer have to fit 'square pegs into round holes'… you'll cut your training time dramatically, have a more cohesive team - and you're guaranteed to save far more than it costs to get the information.

The feedback you get in these reports is priceless. And once you've seen it, if you do have questions, I'll help you understand exactly what it means and how to use the information we've gathered to make a great decision.

Just imagine the good night's sleep you would get - knowing the decision you're making is based on a system that's been proven thousands of times with the biggest companies in the world. All those stressful, emotional, and subjective decisions you've had to make in the past can now be made with a crystal clear understanding of who this person you're about to hire really is.

Imagine how much time, effort, energy and money you would save if you could move your hiring accuracy from where it is now – to 80% or better. What would that be worth to you and your company?

With the right people in place, the culture and performance levels in your company literally change overnight.

GIVE ME 20 MINUTES AND I'LL PROVE IT TO YOU

Recently I've been working closely with large groups of attorneys, podiatrists and dentists from all over the country. Before we get started with measuring the entire organization, I ask them to choose one person in their firm or business they know the most about. I let them put me and my system to the test. If you have a company, I would gladly do the same for you.

That's really the beauty of what I do. Instead of asking you to take my word for it, or trust testimonials from our impressive list of clients – let me prove it to you in less than 20 minutes for FREE.

It doesn't matter who the candidate is. And it doesn't matter where in the world they live, their level of experience, past success or failures, race, or even their cultural biases.

If they're hiding something, you'll know it. If they have the potential to cause problems in your organization, you'll know it. If they have star potential, you'll know it immediately.

Is it perfect? No - we're dealing with human nature. But is it close to perfect? Yes. …As close as you're going to get.

Will it take almost all of the risk out of hiring? Absolutely – because you'll know who and what you're getting *before* you hire them.

I don't tell my clients who to hire unless they want me to. I tell my clients about their candidate's biases. You get more accurate data; then with all you've learned about them - you get to make a much more informed decision.

When clients decide against the data and my expertise - they typically regret it. Invariably, they call to tell me they wish they had paid attention to the information I provide.

My smartest clients tell me they would never think about hiring anyone without calling me first. They call me their *secret hiring weapon* – and I'd love to be yours.

To experience this system yourself – free of charge – and for a free report called *The Seven Most Common Hiring Mistakes Employers Make* - as well as helpful tips to make sure your next hire is your best hire, visit: www.RealTalentHiring.com.

ABOUT JAY

Jay Henderson is the founder of Real Talent, a unique hiring service for bosses who want to know exactly who to hire, what to expect, will they succeed, why, what motivates them and what will they be like in your environment. Jay is one of only 8 Master Certified Consultants in the world using this unique predictive science.

Jay began his corporate training career with the Covey Leadership Center, helping to launch Dr. Covey's best-selling book, First Things First. As a certified instructor of Dr. Covey's three nationally recognized programs: Principle Centered Leadership, 7 Habits of Highly Effective People, and First Things First, Jay has helped many organizations implement Covey Leadership Training.

Since 1993 he has delivered customized training and coaching in leadership, management, marketing and sales development for entrepreneurial businesses nationwide. Real Talent is based in Raleigh, North Carolina, and can be reached at 919-518-2793, by E-mail: RealTalentLLC@Gmail.com, or visit www.RealTalentHiring.com.

CHAPTER 5
DATA: THE HUB OF ALL MARKETING

by Chuck Barnett, Barnett & Murphy Inc.

Sherlock Holmes creator, Sir Arthur Conan Doyle, put these words in his hero's mouth: "I never guess. It is a capital mistake to theorize before one has data. Insensibly one begins to twist facts to suit theories, instead of theories to suit facts."

You can translate that thought directly to address modern marketing. It's also a capital mistake to create a marketing campaign without first having the proper data in place and properly analyzed. Otherwise, you risk twisting the facts to support your marketing, instead of building your marketing around the facts.

Today, we have so much data to work from that it's ridiculous – and ultimately self-defeating – to ignore it. If you do, you end up spending more for fewer results – the exact opposite of what a business seeks to achieve with its ROI. No company should ever waste their time and money on marketing to a person who clearly was never going to buy their product or service in the first place.

Data is the hub around which all other arms of a marketing operation operate. It's always moving, always changing; it feeds all the arms of marketing and, in turn, gets fed back through new leads and generated referrals. And it's the basis of any successful targeted campaign.

MARKETING WITHOUT A NET

I'm grateful for the amount of marketing data that's available to us today, because, in my first job after I obtained my MBA, I went to work for National Liberty Marketing – the largest direct mail insurance company at the time. I was a junior employee who worked in the department dedicated to marketing to current policy holders. We wanted to sell those policy holders higher-priced policies, additional policies and other product. We also were responsible for

41

trying to get past policy holders back in the fold.

The science of this process intrigued me – unfortunately, at that time, there was virtually no science to this kind of direct marketing. This was in the late 80's, when there wasn't the data modeling methodology available that we enjoy today. I was limited to making informed guesses as to what kind of marketing would be effective with these policy holders. Luckily, it was the most profitable division of the company, as we were selling to existing customers with a demonstrated preference for our products – so I had some room to experiment.

Making as much of a science of it as I could, I tried to look for patterns in what <u>was</u> effective. What offer would get the most response? If they didn't purchase for one reason, would another tactic work? I worked on identifying trends and seeing how one element would influence another in ripple campaigns and reapplying methodologies that worked. Hard customer data was hard to come by, so it was more a matter of instinct and broad trend-spotting.

After Liberty, I hooked up with a national marketing agency in Charlotte, North Carolina, where I was first exposed to some sophisticated data models – and real attempts to profile customer data, using MCIF's (Marketing Customer Information Files). This company was able to access more personal information through their dealings with financial institutions - and the beginnings of data modeling were really starting to bloom. It opened my eyes to what could be possible in this field.

DATA FINALLY MAKES THE DIFFERENCE

I was finally able to see those possibilities in action when Jody Murphy, a direct mail colleague of mine and I, formed our own marketing company, Barnett & Murphy Inc. And since our first client was Southeast Toyota, they gave us an incredible opportunity.

Southeast Toyota had spent several million dollars to build a database unparalleled in the business at that time. Since they only operated in five states, they could focus more on individual customers and capture more transactional data on each of them, as well as enhance and profile that data to a greater extent than was being done.

The other innovation I saw from Southeast Toyota was variable printing – being able to, for example, personally address a customer in the body of a letter in a direct marketing piece, instead of just having their name and address on top of the letter. We could also target the mailings in a manner that used to be impossible from a cost standpoint. At the time, they had 18 different car models – and they could now profile each vehicle to see which customer in their new multi-million dollar database would be the most receptive to that particular Toyota model.

This had a huge impact. One vehicle may have only been a good fit for 3% of Toyota's database – and now, technology suddenly made it cost-effective to talk directly to that 3% about that Toyota. And since they had never been marketing to that group personally before, it made a huge difference to sales.

Southeast Toyota is still a great partner of ours and we wouldn't be here without them. They exemplify what we preach to our other clients – a great deal can be done by working with data and applying that data in the most effective way possible in all your marketing endeavors.

THE THREE STEPS TO MAKING DATA DELIVER

As I said at the outset, data is the hub of your marketing efforts. It's who you're selling to – the person who's going to put cash back into your business. What could be more important? And it's every marketer's job to try their best to **sell to the right person at the right time**. The sheer amount of data you can collect these days (it's been said that corporate databases on their customers actually *double* every six months) is mind-boggling and permits businesses now, more than ever, to target the most likely customers at the right moment.

And by the way, if you're saying you don't have a database, I'm willing to bet you're wrong. It could be the names in your accounting file – who you invoice – your Outlook contacts – or just your Christmas card list. Somewhere in your business or your life is a list of contacts - and at least some of those names are completely valid to begin marketing your product or service to. Even if it's just your friends…well, what are friends for?

Whatever state your data is in at the moment, there are three big steps to getting it ready for your next marketing blitz.

1. Practice Good Data Hygiene

Cleaning up your database is the first essential thing you have to do to prepare it for your marketing campaign.

You might think there's nothing wrong with your data – it's perfectly fine and you've used it recently for other marketing purposes. Well, as I also mentioned earlier, data is *always changing*. People move, people get divorced, incomes change – life happens.

First, you'll probably want to ascertain what you're going to do with the data – direct mail, email, telemarketing, whatever means of communication you're going to use. Or, since you're going to work with the data, you may just want to make it as complete as possible for the future. Whatever your needs, determine what information is important and make sure that's as correct as possible.

For instance, you'll need to make sure physical addresses are complete – zip codes, directionals on streets (i.e. North Main, East Broadway, etc.) and that people still live where your data says they live. There are services you can use to check this out for you – and the Postal Service requires that you run your names through their Change of Address database to get your bulk mailing discount.

Or you may just need a first name and an email address – make sure you get that email list cleaned and scrubbed so you're reaching the right person and those email addresses just don't bounce back your way. Whatever your need, it's possible to track these things down in a matter of seconds now, whereas, before online resources existed, it could be a matter of days.

Using a "dirty" database for a marketing campaign means you're either wasting postage on mail that can't be delivered or sending an email that could get bounced back – either way, it's costing you money because you're not reaching your intended prospect. Why send stuff out blind when you can take a little extra time to make sure you're reaching who you want to reach?

2. Enhance Your Data

With your cleaned-up database in hand, now you have a chance to enhance it with other pertinent information – think of it as a DVD loaded with extras. Your customer name, location and email address is the basic "movie" – now you can add on, instead of a director's commentary and a making-of 'featurette', your customer's history, the make-up of their household, what magazines they read, where they shop, etc.

There are more enhancement options available than ever before – and two major companies that provide these kinds of enhancement services are PRIZM, an offshoot of the famous Nielsen research company that provides TV ratings, and PERSONICX. Both of these companies specialize in what's called "market segmentation," which involves studying and breaking down consumer likes, dislikes and buying behavior.

These Data Profiling companies can do more than that as well – they can tell you what a group's influences were growing up, what movies they watch, what websites they visit, the types of vehicles most common in their neighborhoods, etc. You can "cluster-code" certain segments within your data to see what marketing will be most effective to those groups - so even if you don't currently know a lot about your customers, you can find it out pretty fast. And you can find out email addresses, cell phone numbers if you want to do a text campaign, or find out which social networks (Facebook, MySpace) they're involved in.

3. Application Of Data.

You've got all this data – now, the big question is - *what does it mean*? Which segment are the buyers and which are the non-buyers? Is there a portion of non-buyers that can be converted? It's important not just to see who your best customers are, but also the worst – because usually there are some you can legitimately go after and some you should just plain drop from your marketing.

Also, which segment most matches up with what you're selling? If you sell five services and some people already buy two of them, they're a good bet to try and sell one of the other three services to. If someone's already using everything you have to offer, you may just want to offer a "good customer" reward to keep them on board.

It's all in the data – and by reading it correctly, you give your marketing its best possible chance. We all know marketing is always a bit of a gamble – you often don't know when something's going to pay off and when something isn't. Proper data management means you're putting the odds as much as possible in your favor.

If you play the slots at Vegas, you want to know which machine pays off the most. If you're selling your product or service, you want to know which customer is most likely to pay for it. It doesn't mean the machine will give you a jackpot or the customer will buy – it just means **you're playing the odds as best as possible to achieve the best possible outcome**.

So look at what you're going to sell – and how you're going to sell. Match that up to your data profiles as well as you can. And you've increased your chances of success anywhere from 10 to 50%, from what we've seen working with our clients over the years.

DON'T FAIL TO FOLLOW-UP

Data Hygiene, Data Enhancement and Data Application. All important steps – but there is actually another important step after the fact – following up on the results of your marketing. Who bought? Who didn't? What happened that you thought would happen? What was totally unexpected – and how does that impact your business? Now, you're back into hard data, instead of guesswork.

Again, there are many tools to help you analyze the results of your marketing campaign – SAS and SPSS are two major companies that can help you do extensive follow-up with charts and graphs, etc. When I was working at National Liberty, I would have loved to have that kind of data to work with – now, there's so much you can obtain that I actually have to warn against "analysis paralysis," where you end up running so many different data models you forget what you were after in the first place!

Looking at the data carefully in the right way, however, sets you up for the next marketing endeavor with some cold hard facts that should guide you to another successful campaign. You start with data – and you end with data. And that's why I believe it's the most important aspect of any marketing operation.

Not working correctly with data shortchanges yourself and your business – and ultimately your ROI.

MARKETING IN TODAY'S CLUTTERED CLIMATE

We've been fortunate that our current business model allows for a lot of opportunity to work in partnership with our clients. Having a longer-term relationship means we get to know what they really want to accomplish – and can manage the data from start to finish to make sure they get the results they're after.

The important thing to realize moving forward is that consumers are so much more sophisticated than ever before. If you're going to the wrong people in the wrong way in search of a sale, it's not going to happen. Everyone is bombarded by marketing messages – and it's the smart, not necessarily the strong, that cut through the clutter.

Because consumers are so conditioned to marketing, it's more important than ever to get into a permission-based conversation with them. Instead of screaming "Buy!" at them, it's a matter of "We can help you in this way or this way – is that of interest to you?" By taking more of an interactive approach, where consumers feel they have more control in the marketing process, they become a willing participant in it – and you have much more of a chance of a successful sale.

The last thing I'd like to talk about in terms of marketing ROI is …don't forget the power of old-fashioned snail mail. If you're like me, you wake up to ten or twenty marketing emails in your in box – which you quickly delete because you're anxious to get to emails (and work) that matter to your day (hint: if you're going to send out marketing emails, profile when your prospects are actually going to be in front of their computer – there's a much bigger chance your email will be opened if it arrives when the person is already online).

Today, however, real mail stands out – because there's not as much of it. And it's still something you touch, pick up and look at before you decide whether it's worth opening and reading. It's not time to write off real mail yet – as a matter of fact, it's a better time than ever to seriously consider it.

Every one of you spins off dozens of pieces of data when you're going through an ordinary day. And each one of those pieces is picked up by marketing companies and is used to enhance and profile consumers. Every day, increased metrics and measurements are being developed to make data management more sophisticated and specific. Marketers have a great deal more data tools at their disposal as a result; use those tools wisely and you'll have the strongest possible data hub at the center of your marketing operation – as well as a great ROI on every campaign.

ABOUT CHUCK

I want to tell traditional marketers to "Get Your Head Out Of Your Mass!" - which also happens to be the title of the book I'm currently writing and researching.

There is no longer a need - or a place - for mass mailings, bulk generic e-mails or non-customized web landing pages. It's possible to speak to every individual with the offer, images and even language that works best for THEM, yet so few companies are taking advantage and miss the opportunities. You can think of me as an evangelist for Personability!

Chuck Barnett's Specialties:

Marketing, Data Analysis, Public Speaking, Adding Personability (tm) to any marketing campaign to increase ROI, sales and satisfaction!

CHAPTER 6
INCREASE YOUR ROI WITH SMART COPY

by Julie Boswell, Marketing Strategist &
Direct Response Copywriter

There are tons of experts, books, and websites that can teach you the mechanics of writing direct response copy. But in addition to being a science that MUST contain specific elements in order to elicit a response, direct response copywriting, when it's done well, is also an art form. Master that art form and you'll make a lot more money!

What makes copywriting an art form? Copywriting is simply salesmanship in print. And you cannot sell unless you make a connection with your potential buyer. To do that you need to use your imagination and be creative. If you fail to do that … if you're boring, you'll never make any money.

In this chapter, I'll give you a few important tricks that you should implement in ALL of your marketing that will undeniably help you to increase your Return On Investment. It just makes good sense to do these things … thus the title of this chapter, "Increase Your ROI With *Smart* Copy." First, let me tell you how I discovered what really works when it comes to making a lot of money with your marketing.

Over the past 4 years I've helped 'tons' of marketers in all kinds of niches. Remember, it doesn't matter what product you sell, your job as an entrepreneur is to be a "marketer" of that item by creating compelling marketing pieces that make money. I've worked with doctors, lawyers, fitness experts, speakers, real estate investors, hypnotists, martial arts teachers, insurance agency owners, and the list goes on…

I got into all of this in the first place because I had the very good fortune of landing the best job I've ever had. I was the Director of Marketing for Glazer-Kennedy Insider's Circle™ and I worked directly for one of the world's highest paid and most sought after direct response copywriters, Captain Outrageous himself, Bill Glazer. If you're not familiar with Bill and Glazer-Kennedy, you're missing out. Go to www.DanKennedy.com right now and sign up for a free trial membership. You'll be glad you did. Anyway, it was hardly a dream job (I worked my tail off!). My blood pressure will never be the same. But it taught me more about myself and more about being an entrepreneur than I ever expected it to, and I am eternally grateful. It was like getting paid to earn my Masters degree in direct response marketing!

During my time at GKIC, I typically spent 3 or 4 hours a week in a one-on-one meeting with Bill Glazer. We'd talk about all of the marketing that he wanted to do for his businesses and after the meeting I was sent off to implement. It was intense, but again, I wouldn't trade that experience for anything. I hung on to Bill's words and studied his copywriting style. His writing always made a connection with me (more on that later). Eventually, I started offering to take things off his plate and humbly "take a stab" at writing various pieces. After I got a few under my belt, I began taking private client projects on the side while I was still working my fulltime job with Bill. Those side jobs quickly developed into a thriving business that I love. I now work for myself fulltime as a marketing strategist, consultant, and direct response copywriter.

From my time with Bill and from my own experiences of writing and testing marketing pieces, I've learned that there are a few things that really matter when increasing your ROI, no matter what business you're in. And I'm not talking about details like whether you print on yellow or blue paper. Though in some instances, those details do matter, what I have to share with you is more about connecting with your audience as a writer, and then capitalizing on that connection once it's established. Here is what I've learned …

MAKING A CONNECTION

The most important thing you can do as copywriter, or really as a salesman, is to make a connection with your potential buyer. It all starts before you ever put pen to paper. You need to put yourself in the shoes of the person who is opening up the mail. What do they care about? What is important to them? Once you figure that out, EVERY decision you make about how your piece is mailed, what it looks like, what it says, should be made based on what you know about your potential buyer. That may sound like overly obvious advice to you, but you'd be surprised how many businesses fail to do this.

If you take a look at what's inside your mailbox, you'll see very clearly that most marketing is just plain boring. Seriously, whoever is in charge of Geico's (the car insurance company) direct mail campaigns clearly isn't thinking about what's important to me. Their letters always come in a windowed envelope with nothing special showing through the window and it always reveals that it's from Geico. So after a quick glance at the envelope I'm fully aware that it's a solicitation. And while their TV commercials are 'pretty darn' clever, I think it's a huge mistake that they haven't given the Gecko a name.

If they did that, if they named him Harry or Larry or whatever, they could put that name as the return address on the envelope and I might be interested to know why "Larry Green" has sent me a letter. Yes, I know that eventually (the 2nd time I get a letter from him) I'll be able to see that it's from Larry. But hey, that Gecko's got personality. I feel like I know him and I feel like he 'gets' me. I'd much rather get a letter from him than from the Geico Corporation. As it is though, the only action I take after receiving their letters is to put them directly into the trash can, unopened.

So how can you make a connection with your potential customers? I always like to visualize an actual person reading my marketing piece. It's not the same person every time for me since I write for many different industries. But you can very clearly define your audience. For example purposes only, let's say that you market to doctors who own and operate private practices. Paint yourself a detailed picture of one doctor … his name is Paul, age 46, he has 2 kids and is finally getting to the stack of mail that the receptionist put on his desk before he leaves the office for the day. He's in a hurry because he doesn't want to miss dinner with his family again. He wants to sort through the mail and throw out all of the junk, file the bills to be paid, and get the heck out of the office. So, when he comes to your envelope you've got about a half second to stop him in his tracks and get him to care about what you have to say. And remember, you've got to get past the receptionist who probably pre-sorts the mail before 'the doc' ever sees it anyway.

So, make your envelope look very personal - like its coming from a friend. Start your letter with the "so what" information. *Tell him what's in it for him right away.* Don't make him guess. And though you may have a lot of information to give about your offer, make sure the highlights are bigger, bolder, and easy to read, so that at a glance, he can learn everything he needs to know about what you're selling.

You'll find yourself thinking about "Paul" as you make the many decisions that go along with every direct mail endeavor, like whether to use a live stamp or metered postage. And you'll especially think about him as you outline the benefits of your offer. Just the simple act of making your potential buyer a real live human being instead of a list of faceless names will make you a better writer, help you connect with your audience on a personal level, and ultimately increase the response you get from all of your marketing.

MAKING IT EASY

Now that you've got Paul's attention, and he cares about your offer, the most important thing you can do to increase your ROI is to make it really really really easy for him to buy from you.

Provide multiple ways for him to respond to your offer, including:- visiting your website, faxing back a response form, mailing back a response form, and of course, calling a phone number.

I can't stress enough how important it is to provide multiple ways to respond. Nine times out of ten I would choose to respond via the internet. But my husband, who is also an entrepreneur and therefore receives a lot of the same marketing pieces as I do, would almost always want to pick up the phone and speak to a person. Despite my endless efforts to introduce him to the 21st Century's technological advances, he'd be perfectly happy with a rotary phone … and he's only 34! So you see, you just can't predict what method will be the most comfortable for "Paul" to use. He may appreciate a faxable form that he can look over and then hand off to his receptionist to fax back. Then again, he might want less paper in his life and be more apt to visit your website while he 'scarfs down' lunch at his desk. You just never know. So give him options!

TRACK YOUR RESPONSE

Everyone wants to get a better ROI on the marketing that they do, but few business owners are willing to take the time and effort to accurately track the response they get. I'll admit that it's not the easiest thing to do, but there's a lot of money to be made by paying attention to what makes you money. Reread that last sentence and repeat it to yourself every time you spend a dime on marketing.

When it comes to giving out a website, spend the $10 (or less) to buy a domain. You can have your web guy redirect the page to your website, but more importantly, you'll be able to have him track how many hits the page gets. And there is technology available these days (i.e., Google Analytics) that can even tell you how long they stay and what parts of the pages they pay attention to.

Response forms are easy enough to track by printing a unique code on them. The code is simply an internal indicator (for you and your staff) of what response form went with what offer. That way, when they get faxed or mailed back to you, you'll know that they were a result of you making that offer in July (for example) as opposed to when you made it again to the same list in December.

When it comes to listing a phone number in your marketing, use the ROI Guy's call tracking system and you'll automatically capture the information of everyone that calls your office – use the **ROI Bridge** to automatically dump that captured information into your Customer Relationship Management System so it can initiate a follow-up campaign. I can't say enough about the ROI Bridge. It's the best tool there is to help you make the most of every call that comes into your office. Think about how much effort you put into getting "Paul" to call you in the first place. Don't you want to know that he called, when he called, where he called from, and what he called in response to? And don't you want to be able to follow-up with him automatically (meaning without any extra work for you or your staff)?

Knowing all of this information is really the only way that your marketing can get better over time. Armed with this knowledge you'll be able to get to know your potential customer even better, so the art form part of copywriting will come more naturally to you. But the bottom line is that you'll be able to invest in the marketing that makes you more money and forget about the rest. <u>If this response tracking stuff is something that you hate to do, hire someone to do it. It's that important! It can't be skipped.</u>

You've got nothing to lose by implementing the steps I've outlined for you here. Its free to give your potential customer a face and a life of his or her own. …and providing multiple response mechanisms and tracking that response will definitely pay for itself many times over.

Best of luck to you and your business. I hope you've found at least one thing in this chapter that will help to make you a better writer and therefore make you MORE MONEY!

ABOUT JULIE

For nearly 4 years Julie Boswell was the right hand implementer of renowned copywriter and direct response marketer Bill Glazer. As the Director of Marketing for Glazer-Kennedy Insider's Circle she directed and executed ALL of the company's marketing efforts including filling nearly 1,000 seats at their two annual National events, the SuperConferenceSM and the Info-SUMMITSM. She also wrote several very successful campaigns for them including the now famous Roving Reporter campaign which generated over $80,000.00 in sales in just a few days.

Although the content came from Dan Kennedy or Bill Glazer, Julie managed the creation of almost 20 brand new Glazer-Kennedy info-products from artwork concept to packaging and, in some cases, sales copy. While she was at Glazer-Kennedy, she even painstakingly refurbished and updated 10 classic Glazer-Kennedy products, including their marquee resource Magnetic Marketing. Julie knows the process very well and is a valuable asset in the product development aspect of any information marketing business.

Julie now operates her own thriving copywriting and consulting business fulltime, helping all sorts of entrepreneurs grow their businesses through creative and compelling direct response marketing campaigns. She's also developed a comprehensive program to manage info-product creation and launch. To find out more, contact her at julieboswell@gmail.com.

CHAPTER 7
CONNECTING YOUR WAY TO SUCCESS

by Larry Benet, "The Connector"

Not many people get fired for what they do best. But that's just what happened to me in 2006.

I was "selectively outsourced" for *doing too much networking*.

Yes, today I'm known as "The Connector to Billionaires and Millionaires" – but back then, my primary skill only connected me to the unemployment line!

To be fair, my job back then wasn't supposed to be about networking – it's just my natural instinct to do it. And it was a vivid example of the axiom that you should always pursue whatever your passion is. That job had nothing to do with my passion. My current work, however, is *all* about what I love to do best.

Connections. How would any one of us have advanced in life if we didn't connect with certain key people that believed in us, inspired us, taught us and helped us move forward?

Successful people are successful for a reason. I make connections to the kinds of phenomenal personalities that make things happen – I learn from them – and I share their wisdom and techniques with those who connect with me. And I also put in a lot of hours using those connections to help raise money for important international charities that save lives.

Connections are about helping yourself and helping others – and this chapter is about helping you make those connections. I'll be sharing with you some of the secrets that have enabled me to build relationships with some of the best and brightest people in their fields.

CONNECTING TO MY PASSION

I want to return to that time in my life after I lost my job. I was in a very negative frame of mind and not sure what I was going to do with my life. I began to learn from people like motivational guru Mark Victor Hansen in an attempt to find my way.

But it wasn't until I watched the movie "The Secret" – from the bestseller of the same name – that I really made the turn in my own head. As all of you probably already know, "The Secret" is all about deciding what you want and applying a positive focus to that goal. It inspired me to finally drop the negativity, apply that positive focus, and be open to the possibilities in front of me.

A few days later, businesswoman and TV host Merry Miller conducted a seminar with Donald Trump at the Learning Annex, an event that I decided to attend. I had the opportunity to put a question to Mr. Trump, so I asked his advice on how to handle the kind of adversity I had been experiencing. He gave me a very good, thoughtful answer.

But *my* Q & A with the business mogul wasn't the one that stuck with me. It was the exchange he had with the guy behind me. He asked Trump what he would do if he lost all his money?

Trump's answer was delivered without hesitation – "I would be rich. That's all there is to it. Next question."

That was a 'light bulb' moment for me. I realized Trump's belief system in his being wealthy was so strong, nothing could crack it. And I knew I needed that kind of unshakable belief in myself and my ability. I decided that I would focus on building relationships and make that work for me.

I had my first opportunity to put my new plan into action shortly after that. I heard that Virgin CEO Sir Richard Branson would be at a charity event and I made it a point to attend.

I quickly saw that it was going to be incredibly difficult to make the connection I was after. Branson was in the middle of a dance floor, surrounded by security guards, with music blaring so loudly it would be difficult to talk to him. But I managed to get through his entourage and speak to the man himself. I only managed to get 30 seconds to speak to him directly. But by the end of those 30 seconds, I had Sir Richard's email address. And later, to my shock, I realized it was his *private* email address.

What was important about those 30 seconds wasn't the 30 seconds themselves – but *what I had done prior to the event to prepare for them.* I had researched Branson extensively online to see what would be of value to him – and, when I talked to him, I offered a way to help him raise money for his Virgin Homeless fund. In other words, I was giving him something – not asking for something for myself – and it was the beginning of building an important relationship for me.

Some time later, I met Larry King at another charity function. Again, I had done my research on what charity was important to him and spoke to him about helping out. A few days later, I found myself having breakfast with the TV legend in Beverly Hills.

And finally, since good things come in threes, I met the world's 23rd wealthiest man, Bill Bartmann, at another event. I asked him two questions – what was most important to him and what was he the most passionate about? From the discussion that happened as a result of those two questions, I ended up helping him launch his speaking and authoring career, which he's been incredibly successful at.

This was the big turning point for my career – and, in just a little over two years, I've created important connections with such major personalities as Tony Robbins, Jack Canfield, Warren Buffet and many, many more.

HOW DO *YOU* CONNECT?

As I've said, my success began when I developed an unshakable belief system that I could make important connections with powerful people. That gave me the confidence to approach people like Larry King and Sir Richard Branson.

That confidence is important to have. It enables you to have the courage to approach a powerful person – but it's not enough to make the connection you're after. A lot of people approach the rich and famous, but the first reaction of these superstars is usually to be polite but distant. They simply can't handle the overwhelming number of people who want to be close to them.

That's why confidence is only the first step to truly connecting with them. Believing is important – but finding a practical way to build that connection bridge is essential. This is how I make it happen:

- **Find a Way to Make a Personal Connection**

You'll notice I met many of these powerful people at charity events. The trick is to find a venue where you can actually have some "face time" with them – and a fundraiser is an excellent place to do that. Emailing and cold calling these people is a futile endeavor – again, the demands on them are endless. You need to find the opportunity where you can just walk right up to them and have a conversation.

- **Find Out What's Important to Them**

As I did with Sir Richard Branson, you should research the personality you have an opportunity to meet – before that opportunity occurs. Find out what engages them on a personal level – do they have a cause they're passionate about? Chances are they will be attending a charity event precisely because it *is* a cause that they have a large personal interest in.

- **See How You Can Help Them**

Most people approach celebrities because they *want* something from them. That gets very old very fast for them (or anyone else, for that matter – it's why parents get tired!). If, instead, there's some effort or project they're spearheading with which they would welcome some help, that's what you need to focus on.

- **Determine How You Can Add Value**

It's not enough to offer help – you need to determine *exactly what you can do* to help before you encounter the person. What do you have access to that might help them reach a goal? What talents or contacts can you add to the effort? Have specific answers ready.

- **Practice "The Art of the Follow-Up"**

Your objective, when you encounter the person you want to make the connection with, is to leave with a viable way to contact them, as I did with Sir Richard. From there, you have to follow up with the person. They're very busy people, obviously, so you usually have to be persistent – leaving just one message doesn't work.

Leaving a memorable message helps – one I left for a busy executive I know quite well was, "I spoke with God today – how come I can't speak with you???" Of course, a message like that only works if you already have a familiar relationship with the person.

DON'T STOP BELIEVING

By understanding who the people of influence were and how I could add value to them, I've been able to power myself to the top of an industry I just started in a little over two years ago. I also make sure not to ask for something for myself from these important people until long after I've added that value to them.

And again, I will credit my strong belief system. Whether I'm talking to a rich and powerful business CEO or someone just off the street, I always believe I can add value in some shape or form to that person. It may not happen immediately, but I try to make it happen as quickly as possible to cement the bond.

I'd like to give some final advice to every businessperson and entrepreneur out there - to help them keep their belief system strong and keep the kind of the positive focus in place; that's what has helped me achieve so much in so little time.

- **Play to Your Strengths and Focus on Your Passion**

My turning point was deciding to do what I did best – build relationships. You should also work with whatever gifts you have, don't try to force yourself to do something you don't like to do or aren't very good at. Delegate to other people the stuff you don't want to do or can't do very well.

- **Get an Advisory Board of People That Can Help You**

I have a number of coaches I work with to help me get better at what I do. The more associations you build with successful mentors who can help you to the next level, the better off you'll be. You can either try to do it yourself

– and waste time and money on the mistakes you'll invariably make – or you can learn smart, effective short-cuts to achieve what you want from people who have already been through it all. Mentors tell you the quickest way to get where you want to go.

- **Watch Your Words – Watch Your Environment**

Never say you don't have enough money. Never say you can't get what you want. If you're in a negative environment, surrounded by negative people who constantly tell you how you're not going to make it, change it up and find a more positive group to associate with.

- **Don't Watch TV News!**

At least, don't watch too much of it. Yes, I'm serious. Years ago, Ted Turner was so frustrated by the relentless stream of negative stories on the news, he began a weekly show on TBS called "Good News" that ran for many years. If the man who founded CNN thinks TV news is too depressing and downbeat, we should all listen. In general, I firmly believe that the less TV you watch, the more money you'll make.

- **Have Good Systems**

Most entrepreneurs became entrepreneurs because they didn't want to work the 9 to 5 grind. Unfortunately, because they don't implement good systems into their business, they end up working non-stop – and often for less than they'd make in the corporate world. Good systems will help you work less and achieve more.

Connections have blessed me a thousand times over in the past two years – and I hope you have learned something from my successful journey.

Connect with your passion, connect with your dreams, and connect with the people who help you channel that passion and bring your dreams to life.

Believe you can do it – and you will!

ABOUT LARRY

Larry Benet has formed his career around the principle of helping others. He believes the more you give the more you get. He teaches others how to be a VC - VALUE CREATOR. He is known as the Connector, is considered America's Connection Expert, and according to Google is the most connected person on the planet. Google pioneered Pay Per Click Advertising, and Larry pioneered the Pay Per Compliment business model. One of his goals is to raise 1 billion dollars for worthy causes through his connections, his outside the box ideas, and his own money. Another is to eradicate homelessness and poverty in this country and around the world.

Larry has rubbed elbows with President Clinton, Donald Trump, Larry King, and Richard Branson. He has shared the stage with Tony Robbins, Harv Eker, Jay Abraham, Mark Victor Hansen, Jack Canfield, Brian Tracy, Tony Hsieh of Zappos, Paula Abdul, and Jay Leno.

He's helped dozens of clients make connections that helped them find success, skyrocket their income, and reach their dreams. Larry has helped raise money for the Richard Branson Virgin Unite Organization as well as the Larry King Cardiac Foundation. He has served on the board of advisors for the Soul of Africa and the Wyland Foundation and is currently helping We Are the World 2 raise money for the remake of the song made famous by the likes of Lionel Richie, Stevie Wonder, Alicia Keys, Bruce Springstein, John Mayer, and many others. This project will raise money for Africa.

CHAPTER 8
GIVING DIRECT MAIL PERSONALIZED POWER

by Lee Weiner, Owner CEO, Devin Herz, CCO and Scott Strepina, Business Development, The Print Concierge

magine someone standing by your mailbox, going through your mail and throwing out everything that person thought you didn't really need to see.

No, that's not a component of the Patriot Act that you didn't know about – but it is a fair comparison to what spam filters do to email inboxes. They flag marketing emails and, for the most part, either stop them 'in their tracks', or dump them in your spam folder, where you trash them later.

On the other hand, it's *illegal* to interfere with any mail that's sent through the U.S. Postal System to your home mailbox. And it would be downright creepy to have anybody sifting through your physical mail before you had a chance to do so.

That's one very big reason direct mail still works – and why it will for the foreseeable future. Yes, email marketing is an almost no-cost venture – but you can't be sure those emails will ever reach their intended destinations.

Even if the spam filter doesn't stop it, there are other obstacles – such as someone changing their email address, leaving you with no idea how to track down that individual again. In contrast, the U.S. Postal Service keeps track of who moves and to where – and makes that information available to direct mail marketers.

Direct mail has always been an incredibly effective and creative tool that marketers have relied on for decades and decades. It continues to be even more so now – thanks to new technological breakthroughs that allow us to personalize each campaign to amazing new levels, track the delivery of every mailing, and to bring the recipient back online to a personalized web page that has an incredible conversion rate.

Yes, Old Media and New Technology can make an awesome combination – and our company, **The Print Concierge**, has made every effort to stay out in front of all the exciting cutting-edge developments in direct mail. In this chapter, we're going to share a few secrets about how you can radically raise your ROI and response rates for direct mail campaigns through the use of these new tools.

THE POWER OF PERSONALIZATION

Although our core business is commercial printing, **The Print Concierge** is your direct marketing partner and serves as the marketing leg of your business helping with strategizing, design, development and printing of successful marketing efforts. We always strive to develop an in-depth understanding of your business, your goals and your targeted audience – and then use this knowledge to help develop marketing initiatives that demonstrably grow your business.

This, of course, extends to our direct mail services. We offer a wide variety of these services, all under one roof, so we can stay with a project from start to finish. This includes everything from consultation, graphic design, copywriting, package consultation, and data services, to printing and delivery. Our vision is to continually evolve to meet or exceed the needs of our clients' business today and tomorrow.

Part of that vision involves using the newest technologies in the most creative and impactful ways possible. With the latest digital printing equipment and accompanying software we have on hand, the possibilities are now endlessly exciting.

For the direct mail marketer, most of that excitement focuses on how easily it is to personalize their campaigns to individual customers with innovative new techniques. *Variable Data Printing* (VDP) makes that possible. And the excitement from a marketing standpoint comes from the fact that VDP has been proven to boost Direct Mail response rates by *double* to *triple* digits.

So why isn't everyone taking advantage of this technological breakthrough in printing? Because not everyone is aware of the incredible versatility of digital printing. Yes, VDP has been around for awhile – how many years ago did you start getting Publisher's Clearing House letters with your name in giant type on a phony million-dollar check? But now the technology has gone so far past being able to just print a prospect's name on a marketing piece that it's incredible.

Our advanced form of on-demand printing enables you to grab the attention of each recipient with more impact than ever before. Every element on every piece, including text, graphics, and photographic images, can be customized to your exact specifications.

And we aren't just talking names either – VDP technology now allows us to personalize a mail campaign with whatever customer data you might want to use in each mailing.

For example, one of our clients, a Glazer-Kennedy Insider's Circle member, runs a sewing machine and vacuum cleaner business in New Jersey. They wanted to contact customers who had bought sewing machines from them and remind them to bring them in for maintenance.

The direct mail piece was personalized through the latest digital photography, so that each customer's first name appeared to be spelled out with thread. Then, because the company had the date when each customer purchased their sewing machine stored in its database, that information was also, through VDP technology, placed in the mailing.

So, suppose your name was Joe Smith and you bought a sewing machine on March 4th, 2008. You would have received a mailing that read, "Joe, remember when you bought your sewing machine from us on March 4th, 2008?", and then went on to remind you to have the sewing machine serviced.

This campaign was an amazing success – with 2300 people out of 7000 total mailings signing up for the servicing at $100 a pop. But its success wasn't just because of the VDP – the direct mail campaign also had a *PURL* component.

And if you don't know what a *PURL* is…we're about to tell you.

THE PURL – THE JEWEL OF ANY DIRECT MAIL CAMPAIGN

The power of personalized direct mail has been proven to raise response rates into the double digits, as we've already mentioned. Add in the power of a PURL – a Personalized URL that's provided to the direct mail recipient for their response – and you create a potent 'one-two personalized punch' that:

1. Boosts *conversion* rates into the double digits (normally unheard of in the direct marketing world)
2. Allows the business to build a new database of warm and hot leads, and
3. Provides instant tracking of recipient responses to the direct mail piece

With all those positives…why not do a *PURL*?

*PURL*s were created back in 2006 when direct mail marketers discovered that almost half of direct mail respondents were taking their direct mail marketing piece right over to the computer to respond and complete the transaction. This was surprising news, and something that obviously could be leveraged to help boost response and conversion rates.

By giving customers their own *PURL* in a direct mail piece, they could go online to a special web page that addressed them by name and provided an enticing "Call to Action" – all-in-all, a tremendous way to boost the ROI of any campaign for the above three reasons.

As we already mentioned, the sewing machine direct mail campaign provided exactly that kind of *PURL* element. As the customer's name was actually in the URL provided by the company, it was exciting for the customer to go to the computer and check out the *PURL* to see what it's all about – and no doubt contributed to the high response/conversion rate of that particular campaign.

The software we use to generate the *PURL* automatically personalizes it through the name provided in the URL – and provides a way to immediately track whoever visits the website. Therefore, you can collect the info on warm leads (those who merely visit the *PURL*) as well as the info on hot leads (those who actually fill in the requested information on the *PURL* to respond to the offer). You no longer have to wonder who's responding, because the *PURL* automatically provides real-time instant measurement whenever one of your prospects visits their webpage.

If you follow the rules of a true direct mail campaign, and stick to a schedule of consistent mail drops, there's no reason you shouldn't see double-digit response rates. Another one of our clients, a dentist, recently sent out two mailings through us to 1000 people – and around 200 of those prospects visited their individual PURL web pages, for a 20% response rate. Again, an incredible percentage for a direct mail campaign response.

By the way, there's still one more way you can boost that response rate even higher. The Post Office is now making IMB (*Intelligent Mail Barcode*) technology available to direct mail marketers. By placing this barcode on each piece of mail, we are suddenly able to achieve total tracking of mail sent out.

In other words, we can track when a specific prospect receives one of our mailings. That means if you receive a direct mail piece on a certain day, we'll know it. Then, we can email you to say a special mailing was delivered to you today and don't forget to visit your *PURL* – and then we'll have the *PURL* link embedded in the email so you can just click through to it. This provides an awesome 'no-to-low-cost' follow-up to the mailing.

All these hi-tech breakthroughs are incredible assists to any direct mail campaign – but it all starts with the right creative approach and the proper marketing techniques. At **The Print Concierge**, we help our clients make the most of direct mail pieces, from conception to delivery to actual customer response.

QR CODES (QUICK RESPONSE)

We also continue to explore the latest technological advances to determine how they can help our clients. While QR codes have been a marketing mainstay for over 3 years now in Japan we are starting to see them pop up in the states. Recently Facebook as well as Google have been toying around with QR codes which is a strong sign that this technology will be more prevalent in the near future.

We are seeing this type of marketing being used on posters in shop windows and now direct mail. Early adapters of this technology include the mobile tech niche and we fully expect this to capture attention in a broader scope of niches as QR Codes become more commonplace.

QR Codes are the next step in combining attention-getting online technology with great proven print marketing campaigns.

This is no time to abandon the power of direct mail marketing – because it is a time where you can enhance that power and take it to incredible new heights.

ABOUT THE PRINT CONCIERGE: LEE, DEVIN AND SCOTT

The Print Concierge serves as your collaborative partner in print, design and marketing. We will develop an in-depth understanding of your company, your goals – and your targeted audience. Using this knowledge, we will help you develop marketing initiatives that demonstrably grow your business and improve ROI.

Our clients range from small start up ventures to Fortune 500 corporations.

Projects also vary dramatically in size and complexity. For example, we handle jobs as basic as printing business cards to those involving sophisticated orchestration of highly customized Variable Data Printing with PURL (Personalized URL) enhancement.

Our inherent flexibility has enabled us to successfully manage and deliver million-plus runs, enrich fine art catalogs, and provide fabricated casino boat signage. It also facilitates small print runs or one-offs of highly customized materials for single events or engagements.

Regardless of the scope of the assignment, each client receives individual attention. A project manager will oversee your job from start to finish. Our primary mission is to exceed your expectations, expand your market share and to do it all at a surprisingly low cost.

You will also enjoy the services of a full range of creative talent, including print experts, graphic designers, copywriters, photographers and web developers. They can help you gain a competitive edge through focused creativity. In fact, our staff recently won an ADDY Award for excellence in the world's largest advertising competition. While The Print Concierge was gratified to be recognized over 60,000 other entries, our true satisfaction came from the impressive results enjoyed by our client in new revenue.

CHAPTER 9
MONTHLY CUSTOMER NEWSLETTERS
THE SECRET TO MORE PROFITS AND CUSTOMERS FOR LIFE

by Jim Palmer, The Newsletter Guru

Warning! This chapter contains phenomenal information on how to grow your business and boost your profits with a monthly customer newsletter. But you should also know that I'm also going to challenge you throughout not to be what I call: *a newsletter pansy!*

Based on my nearly 30 years' experience in marketing and growing businesses with newsletters, both for my previous employers and now for my hundreds of clients and customers in seven different countries, I am 100 percent confident that if you follow my advice and suggestions and are not *a newsletter pansy*, you <u>will</u> see more profits and customers-for-life in your business—<u>no matter what business you are in!</u>

My belief in friendly customer newsletters as an amazing—almost magical—marketing tool is so strong that in 2001, when I decided to go into business for myself, I knew that newsletters would be my main offering. And what a ride it's been!

My belief in friendly customer newsletters is so strong that I believe anyone who doesn't mail a monthly newsletter to customers is simply being *a newsletter pansy*. There is simply too much empirical evidence and data that prove my case.

It's a fact that customer newsletters help businesses succeed. And the best and most effective way to grow your business, boost your profits, and get more customers for life is to <u>mail monthly.</u> Anything less frequent than monthly means that you are simply being *a newsletter pansy*!

Bill Glazer, the president of Glazer-Kennedy Insider's Circle, says this about newsletters: "Who should be sending out newsletters to their customers, clients, patients, and prospects? The answer is everybody! That's right; there is not a business on the planet that couldn't benefit 'BIG TIME' with a monthly company newsletter. There is no better way to develop a relationship with people than sending out a properly written newsletter."

Dollar for dollar, newsletters are the most effective marketing tool available. Plus, customers who read your newsletter are usually in a good position to do business with you again, and recommend your product or service to others. And that's where your new business comes from! Let me share with you more of what I call the magic of newsletter marketing.

Newsletters are not perceived in the same manner as are postcards, fliers, or other forms of direct mail marketing. When people receive these or anything else that has a sales and marketing feel to it, their guard goes up and they think, "Uh-oh. What are they trying to sell me?"

Newsletters work well because they tend to be read as informational, making them more welcome when they are received. As such, they have higher readership than other forms of advertising. People also tend to be more receptive to what you have to say in your newsletter, because newsletters aren't meant to be sales tools. Rather, they are designed to be a resource.

Marketing genius Dan Kennedy put it this way: "People are conditioned to be less resistant to reading information such as articles than they are advertising." Because people are conditioned to be less resistant to reading information, which is exactly what a newsletter should be, most people read a newsletter with their guard down. This is a HUGE marketing advantage. When your customers' guard is down, they are open and receptive to what you have to say!

A customer newsletter is the strongest marketing and business-building tool available—bar none. Newsletters open doors.

That is the magic of why newsletters are such an effective marketing tool—people don't realize that they're actually reading something that's going to cause them to buy...if the newsletter is done correctly. That's the big caveat here. To learn more about creating a great newsletter that gets results, I invite you to get a copy of my book, *The Magic of Newsletter Marketing—The Secret to More Profits and Customers for Life*! This book will help you; it's the 'wand' that will open doors and bring you customers.

Now I want to share with you seven of the many proven ways that newsletters will help your business grow.

Secret 1. Newsletters Help Keep Customers

Your current customers hold the best prospects for future growth. Plus, the longer they are customers, the more likely they are to spend with you.

A monthly company newsletter helps you stay 'top-of-mind' with your current customers. When your newsletter arrives, your customers start to think about you. Issue after issue, your newsletter reinforces your relationship with your customers, and gives you a way to tell them about products and services they may not know about.

Secret 2. Newsletters Help Get New Customers

You want your newsletter to help you get new customers. Informative articles give your newsletter what marketing pros call "pass-along value." Your newsletter makes it easy to pass on the information. Because people read newsletters as a publication and not as a marketing piece, a newsletter is a great way to tell potential customers about your business.

Secret 3. Newsletters Help Build Credibility

When people read your brochure, they treat it as a piece of marketing literature. But when they read your newsletter, they treat it as a publication. Your newsletter also gives you the opportunity to tell people success stories about what you do and how well your products work. You can illustrate the benefits of your product or service with statistics and customer testimonials.

Credibility is a huge benefit of a monthly printed newsletter. Listen to what Nick Nanton, the celebrity lawyer and best-selling author of *Celebrity Branding You,* says: "I didn't believe it either. But adding a hard-copy newsletter to my business was the best thing I ever did. It increased my credibility, visibility, and profitability virtually overnight. If you don't have a newsletter, you're making a huge mistake by missing the opportunity to develop a deeper relationship with your prospects and clients for maximum profitability."

Secret 4. Newsletters Help You Stand Out from Your Competition

Since you decide the direction and content of each newsletter, you can differentiate yourself from others—especially the larger businesses that typically do not produce customer newsletters.

Secret 5. Newsletters Enhance Your Reputation

Your customers may not be ready for or need your product or service today, but when they are, they want an experienced professional. People want to do business with someone they know, like, and trust, so when they are ready for what you offer, they'll turn to you.

Secret 6. Newsletters Help You Build Your Brand

Branding is the art of making people aware of who you are, what you do, and how you're different from and better than the competition. You want to have a little bell 'go off' in people's heads when they hear your name. You want them to say, "Oh, yes, they're the people who…"

When your newsletter is delivered at the same time each month, it builds up a level of importance. It helps build your brand, which helps your business grow.

Secret # 7. Newsletters Have A Longer Shelf Life Than Other Types Of Marketing

Newsletters are portable; they go everywhere. Newsletters that are informative, fun, and easy to read are not thrown away. People pass along newsletters to friends, business associates, or even neighbors. This is a *huge* benefit of producing a newsletter.

The question many people ask is, "Why publish a customer newsletter every month?" If nothing I have written so far makes any sense, let me give you a little straight talk. The reason that you mail your customers a print newsletter every month is because it works! **It works 'BIG TIME'!**

Publishing a customer newsletter every month is simply the right thing to do for your business. Just like changing the oil in your car every three thousand miles. It's the right thing to do. When you change the oil in your car, you don't see or feel any immediate gratification—you do it because it will make your car last longer and serve you better.

It's like that with a newsletter. You publish a newsletter every month because it's the right thing to do for your business. Much of the time you won't see any immediate gratification. Customers may not mention that they like your newsletter, and you may not hear your cash register ring more often immediately after mailing it. But it is the right thing to do for your business, and doing so month in and month out, like clockwork, is the surest way I know to boost your profits and get more customers for life.

To ignore this reality and do anything less is being *a newsletter pansy* and potentially harming your business.

Here's what I know about newsletter marketing from almost thirty years of experience. The companies that publish a monthly newsletter, month-in and month-out, like clockwork, have stronger, longer-lasting, and more profitable relationships with their customers and clients. And, as history has shown, they have more repeat and referral business. Let me again quote marketing legend Dan Kennedy, who says in his book, *NO B.S. Direct Marketing*, "My single biggest recommendation is the use of a monthly customer newsletter. Nothing, and I mean nothing, maintains your fence better." Again, publishing a monthly customer newsletter is simply the right thing to do—so don't be *a newsletter pansy*!

You might be wondering why I suggest that you focus so much of your time and effort on current customers rather than on new customers. I'm glad you asked. Let me introduce you to Jim Palmer's 80/20 Rule of Marketing …

No doubt you've heard of the 80/20 rule that says 80 percent of your profits come from 20 percent of your customers. I believe that, and so should you—it's the truth. I contend that smart entrepreneurs and business owners should focus more of their marketing, time and resources on nurturing, developing, and growing the customer relationships that they already have, instead of constantly trying to acquire new customers. It costs more and takes longer to acquire and sell to a new customer than it does to sell more to current customers.

Most businesses spend the majority of their marketing time and resources trying to acquire *new* customers. That makes no sense. It is so much easier and quicker to sell more to your current customers.

So the right thing to do is to spend a majority of your marketing dollars continuing to grow, and maximize the profitability of these existing customer relationships. You already have an established relationship with your current customers, and they have already purchased from you. This means that they find value in what you're selling and they trust you. This is a huge hurdle that we all have to overcome when we are prospecting for new customers—a hurdle that you've already overcome with your current customers.

So now that you've gone to the time, effort, and expense of acquiring these customers, the right thing to do for your business is *to maximize the profitability* of your customer relationships.

A monthly customer newsletter helps you stay top-of-mind with your current customers. Your newsletter arrives, and instantly your customers are thinking about you. After receiving your newsletter on a consistent basis, your customers actually begin to look forward to receiving it—it's a welcome friend— and they are curious to see what tips and stories you are sharing with them in the newest issue.

Issue after issue, your newsletter reinforces your relationship with your customers. It makes your fence stronger. It gives you a way to tell current customers about products and services you provide that they may not know about.

So there you have it—I simply can't say it any more clearly! **Publishing a monthly customer newsletter is smart.** Not doing so, no matter what business you're in, is simply being *a newsletter pansy*.

You may be asking, "If newsletters are such a powerful marketing tool, then why doesn't every business use one?" I'm glad you asked; that's an easy question to answer.

The fact is, newsletters can be difficult and time consuming to produce. That's why most companies that say that they have a "monthly" newsletter send it out...*only three to four times per year!*

When asked why they don't do it more consistently, the top two reasons given are:

1. They take too long to produce.
2. I'm always struggling to find content (what to put in the newsletter).

Perhaps this may be why you are not yet sending your customers a monthly newsletter, following the successful and proven path to growth and higher profits that so many before you have. Am I right? And let's face it—as entrepreneurs, we're already wearing many other hats, and when 'push comes to shove', the newsletter always seems to get 'pushed to the back burner' or, worse yet, 'completely off the stove'!

If this has been your experience and what has been holding you back, I invite you to check out my wildly popular "Done-for-You" newsletter program called **No Hassle Newsletters**. Every month, I provide subscribers with ready-to-go newsletter templates and a huge assortment of my famous customer-loving™ content. Learn more at www.NoHassleNewsletters.com.

So, now it's up to you. What you do with the information I've shared in this chapter is entirely your decision. Only you can take action to get and keep more customers now. Only you can take action to build healthier, stronger relationships with your customers, clients, and prospects. Only you can begin to boost your profits by doing more repeat and referral business with your current customers! I'll conclude this chapter as I started, with a challenge.

I challenge you to start or restart your monthly customer newsletter now—and to continue. Now go do it, and don't be a ***newsletter pansy***!

Oh, and by the way, you may have noticed that I did not discuss e-mail newsletters, or e-zines, in this chapter. If you want to know my feelings about e-zines and their proper place in your marketing arsenal, read my book!

But let me just leave you with this quick thought about whether an e-zine has the same perceived value as a print newsletter. The next time Mother's Day or perhaps your spouse's birthday comes around, send an e-card instead of a $5 Hallmark card and see what kind of a reaction you get. You tell me if he or she feels appreciated. You tell me if he or she feels as though you placed a high value on the relationship. If and when you try this experiment and you get a little "static" about the e-card, shoot me an e-mail and let me know if you're called 'a greeting card pansy'!

ABOUT JIM

Jim Palmer is an entrepreneur, author, speaker, and consultant. Jim is internationally known as The Newsletter Guru, the go-to resource for smart, effective strategies that maximize the profitability of customer relationships, and he is the acclaimed author of *The Magic of Newsletter Marketing—The Secret to More Profits and Customers for Life.* His companies include No Hassle Newsletters, NewsletterPostcards.com, The Newsletter Guru's Concierge Print and Mail on Demand Service, The Newsletter Guru's StandOUT E-zines, and Super Affiliate Pages. For a free newsletter template, 20-page special report, and more information on Jim and his companies, visit www.TheNewsletterGuru.com.

CHAPTER 10
MAXIMIZING RADIO ADVERTISING ROI

by Harmony Tenney, MBA

I didn't set out to be one of the world's greatest radio advocates. When I was hired as a radio rep, other reps were sharing their testimonials and success stories. I took them with a grain of salt. As I began putting radio in place for my clients, I started hearing their success stories and started seeing the power of radio and what it can do for companies all across many different industries. I was so excited because radio allowed me to take an investment from a business, put it through a process, and bring it back to the business owner in sale-after-sale-after-sale. I'm continually surprised every day at what a wonderful miracle radio is. Some of my clients experienced double digit growth!

My favorite experience is having companies coming back to me saying "Oh my gosh, this works so well ! Let's put more money into it and see how much more we can get of the market." I've found that my personal niche is clients that are maybe 40 years in business or longer, or 2nd or 3rd generation businesses. It's a wonderful group to work with, because not only have they heard and seen it all, they can 'spot a phony' miles away. They also have a good sense of what it takes to invest to bring back a good return. That's all been really helpful as I go through the process with them of developing a radio campaign, bringing together all of the elements that we can to push it to the next level, and then watching the sales come in and repeating the process.

Radio advertising, when done well, is akin to direct mail 'on steroids'. Really. Radio reaches 96% of the U.S. population weekly, with 92% of the listenership remaining through the ads that play: (www.RadioAdLab.com). Each station is deliberately "programmed" to attract a specific age and gender demographic, so that it can attract specific advertisers and deliver results to them (in the form of increased sales). It does so by utilizing differing "formats." News Talk listeners differ from Lite Rock listeners – both in their age and interests. This works in your favor, and brings your investment greater efficiencies. Because of radio's demographic and psychographic targeting, a dollar invested in advertising on specific stations (even specific hours of a particular station) can be as powerful as investing $1.30, $1.70, even $4.00 spent on another medium. Making dollars work harder is always in your best interest. Radio advertising allows you to pick a station that mirrors your very best customers, and immediately attract more just like them, while spending fewer dollars !!

Radio advertising investments should be approached as if you are hiring a sales rep for your company that knocks on thousands, tens of thousands, even millions of doors weekly. Radio ads are the ultimate "warm" sales call, because listeners consider the products and services advertised on their station as something offered personally to them (especially when voiced by station DJs). Ads that air on a radio station receive a subliminal "thumbs up" by listeners, as if the station and its DJs are personally recommending the goods or services named in the ads. Radio also removes objections, while establishing your business as a known quantity with the qualities of viability, trustworthiness and caring. Radio is the ultimate 'word-of-mouth', in that you decide what is said, to whom it is said, and how often they hear about you.

However, radio advertising is also one of the most challenging mediums. Not many know what works, what doesn't, and how to make radio yield a 'bumper crop' of prospective and profitable customers year after year. It's a goldmine in that radio is particularly gifted at targeting groups and delivering salient information. However, many small business owners and entrepreneurs have been burned by following the advice of their radio station's rep. Therefore, 'going back in the water' is never easy for those burdened by invoices that just keep coming, especially if a contract was non-cancelable. Painful wallets from the past often overpower the simple truth that radio removes consumer objections, and warms prospective customers to a state of having "heard about you" – all positive, *thanks to your ads*.

Making it work. Start by asking your current customers what their three favorite radio stations are. This will help you find a few stations to test. Make sure you're asking your best customers, and not the 'nickel and dime' folks. Choose a station that reaches your target demo (men, women, affluent, multicultural, various age groups, etc), covers your preferred service area (can be neighborhood specific, state specific, large or small), and gives you correct frequency, (the number of times listeners are offered their chance to respond to your ads) from within your budget. It's important that you don't just pick the station you regularly listen to. You are NOT your customer, and you can 'flush' a lot of money away by choosing a station that you prefer, rather than one your customers prefer.

An important note: radio divides each 24 hour day into several 4 to 5 hour segments: Morning Drive, Midday, Afternoon Drive, Evening and Overnight. You should ask the station rep what time of day the station has the most listeners in your target group (the answer is NOT always drive time). Ask for ratings information, hour-by-hour listening charts for your target demographic, and client testimonials. Once you receive the requested reports, make sure that they are indeed for your target group, and not for some generic "adults 12+" or "25+" or some group other than the one you have targeted.

Building a solid schedule is pretty simple - make sure you "own" one or two dayparts weekly. If you've chosen a music station, try 2 ads per day for five weekdays during one 4 hour period **_OR_** 3 per day for at least 3 weekdays during a single 4 or 5 hr period. **_THEN ADD_** another set of either of the above, making 18 – 20 ads per week. If you're advertising on a news / talk / sports station, you'll need to make sure you have ads on all but one hour of the show, daily, so that the listeners get to know you and associate your business with the show. Make sure you're advertising at least two weeks per month. Decide whether you'd like to advertise the first and third weeks, or the second and fourth weeks. Later, test two weeks in a row, or advertising three weeks of the month. (Testing means that you try a different schedule for three months, then compare the results to those obtained by your first schedule. Continue with the one that yielded better, and begin again - <u>trying each time to beat your best-resulting-schedule-to-date</u>).

Next, build some frequency into your schedule by checking for special programming, such as a feature or call-in show, that would be relevant to your particular business. A feature is a news, weather, sports, or traffic update, a snapshot of upcoming events in your community, the day's celebrity / entertainment update, etc) Then, find out what "extras" are available, such as bonus ads, streaming ads or inclusion of your logo and link on the station's website.

Offer to give gift certificates, products and / or services away on-air for station contests. Don't count yourself out of promotional participation on a station just because you can't figure out how it would work. Ask for the rep's help. You can give away promotional items, a free copy of a book you've written, a certificate for 'dinner for two' at a nice restaurant, or Visa gift cards. It's also important to note that the person receiving the giveaway is NOT what matters. The reason to do giveaways is that your business gets mentioned to those same listeners you are advertising to - they're already familiar with you !!

Finally, ask what community events the station is involved with that would be of interest to your customers, and any that mirror your own personal charitable-giving preferences. Choose one, two or three in which you'll proudly participate. Then, promote your participation heavily to your own customers, and invite your customers to participate as well.

Crafting what is actually said in your ad is important. Do not just put your print ad on the air. And avoid clichés in your ads – they bore listeners to death. Do not just use an ad the rep provides (most reps DO NOT write their own ads, have never studied ad writing, and hate to do it). Instead, choose to include only what will help prospective customers become your best customers. Begin with a Promise / Benefit introductory statement - what you are offering and what it means to the listener (how it fits in and improves their lives). This grabs attention and sparks interest. Include your tagline and how the listener can reach or meet you. Then, in three sentences, share how your promise / benefit is possible. With each one, draw another bridge from the listener to your offerings. Repeat the Promise / Benefit introductory statement, the company name, tagline and locator information, then conclude with a call to action.

QUICK TIPS:

1. Always use sixty second ads. Thirty second ads don't give you the time or opportunity to share what strong sixty second ads do. Studies show that listeners cannot tell the difference between thirty second ads and sixty second ads, so use all the time available to you.
2. Make sure also to air only one ad at a time – NEVER rotate more than one ad, unless you have a high frequency schedule for each ad. Having two ads rotate on one schedule dilutes your frequency and your ROI (that is, it wastes your money).
3. Run your ads six to eight weeks before you change them. (Once you get sick of hearing them, keep them on at least three more weeks).

Voicing the ad is easy. Stations produce ads for free, and the most loyal listeners perceive the DJs as family. However, you should test to determine if an "out of the area" voice gets more response than one the loyal listeners are used to. Should you pay for an endorsement by an on-air talent ? It's not usually worth it. Please do note that even "live read" ads are scripted. As for music - it's a great way to set an emotional tone for your business - stick to the same music for years at a time. You might even consider purchasing a jingle - just make sure it does not overpower nor take away from your message in any way. Beware of "generalities" in a jingle - pithiness is priceless.

You might think that once you actually begin airing your ad that your work ends... not true! The start of the airing is only the culmination of the pre-work necessary to begin the profit-building momentum of your campaign. Tracking your responses is the next, and critical, step. Using Excel☐, or your contact / database management system, note each contact received (call, walk-in, email, etc.) along with the date and time. Ask how the respondent heard about your business. Note the city and state of the respondent's residence (if you're advertising out of state, ask if they have recently traveled in the area you're advertising in), ask their three favorite radio stations (to provide future station ideas for testing and market expansion). Finally, total up the number of calls received, number of walk-ins, number of website hits, etc, for each day, week and month – and cross-reference your responses with the days, times and weeks you advertise.

Please note that in today's 'sea of information' and information access, people can look up your phone numbers, your web address, your name and business - in any number of ways. Make sure you ask each caller, web visitor and respondent how they heard about you. Your radio ads will boost any other advertising that you do, so refer back to your baseline to see the effect of your radio advertising on all the means of contact you have in place, for your business.

Beware – once you actually begin advertising, every rep in the area (TV, Radio, Outdoor Billboard, etc.) will come knocking on your door or calling in via phone. "Monitoring" other media is an essential part of all reps prospecting methodology. If you have a radio consultant, you can just direct these reps there. Your consultant will be versed in the goals of your business and will be able to judge compatibility, and if desired, a "test" campaign. It's best to simply say "we're not interested," which will save a lot of time and energy, and maintain strategic focus. (You <u>must</u> resist the curiosity to invest time with what might or might not happen if you use medium #2 or #3).

Finally, having one key person designated to oversee the campaign, either in your business or a consultant outside of it, will allow you to keep up with the tracking, analysis of resulting data, and recommendations for your next moves (testing / increasing market share).

ABOUT HARMONY

Harmony Tenney is an Independent Radio Consultant, competent in both branding and direct-response radio advertising methods. In 2006, Radio Ink Magazine recognized her as a Top Ten National Finalist for Account Executive of the Year. She has helped small business owners in many industries achieve double digit growth through profitable marketing initiatives - even in flat markets. Her clients call her "The Profit Panther," and both her undergrad and graduate classmates voted her **Most Likely to Appear on the Cover of Business Week**. Ms. Tenney offers her clients a guarantee and proven results from her "Powerfully Profitable, Done-for-You Radio Advertising." She also offers several info products for businesses seeking to utilize Radio Advertising most effectively in their marketing campaigns. Reach Harmony at: 540-255-5686, or by email: Harmony@ RadioAdvertisingGenius.com.

CHAPTER 11
MARKETING...A LOVE STORY

by Nina Hershberger, Director of Results,
Megabucks Marketing

F irst of all, thanks to Richard for giving me the opportunity to tell my story. I should probably start by introducing myself. My name is Nina Hershberger – but chances are you don't know me by that name. Chances are, you know me as the internationally famous **Wallet Mailer Lady**.

And for good reason. My company, Megabucks Marketing, sends out hundreds of thousands of wallet mailers every year for clients all over the world. It's one of the most popular and successful direct marketing pieces out there. So while there's a lot more to me than wallets made out of paper, stuffed with fake money and sales letters, I actually consider being known as the *Wallet Mailer Lady* something of an honor.

Sample of our famous wallet mailer
www.wallet-mailer.com

Because it means I've made a name for myself – even if it isn't *my* name – doing what I love more than anything in the world. And that's marketing.

IN THE BEGINNING...

As far back as I can remember, marketing was really the only thing that made my toes tingle and my heart race. To me, seeing a great marketing campaign was better than climbing to the top of the Eiffel Tower, or looking at the Mona Lisa, or eating a chocolate soufflé...although the soufflé would be a close second.

There was absolutely no question – marketing was my true calling in life. It was the only thing I could imagine myself doing. I majored in marketing at Indiana University. Like most college students, I didn't have a clue where I'd work or what exactly I'd be doing, but marketing fascinated me.

Maybe subconsciously my love affair with marketing started at a young age, when I begged my parents to let me go door-to-door selling rusty bobby pins - they said "no" – but later I did sell Christmas cards and Avon door-to-door and peddled newspapers for 5 years.

Marketing is a "learning by doing" kind of job. You can't really grasp the 'ins and outs' of making that unique connection between a buyer and a product or service by listening to a bunch of professors talk in a classroom. Especially since those professors are *in the classroom*, not out in the real world - testing and trying and seeing what works and what doesn't.

That dream job where I was able to do the thing I loved most didn't materialize instantly. But I was an adult and a college grad. I needed to work. So I started 'temping' and discovered that in addition to marketing, I had a real knack for technical stuff. Did it make my heart race and my toes tingle? Not exactly, … but it did pay the bills!

I wound up in the corporate world at The Associates, a 50 billion dollar a year finance company that was eventually acquired by Citicorp. And while it wasn't what you would call a passionate relationship, The Associates and I did hit it off. I was promoted five times in seven years, eventually rising to the rank of Director of Output Services.

(Which, in English, means I was in charge of printing.)

I should have been satisfied. I was on my way to a brilliant career. But I didn't just miss marketing. I *needed* it. I needed to stretch my brain and make those connections between people and seeing the results.

I assembled a team of the best tech people, designers and operators in our firm. Once they were in place, it was my turn. I began to market our print and mail services to different departments all over the company. My marketing strategy *worked.* We went from one slower digital printer to four high speed digital printers producing 9 million direct mail pieces per month by the time I left five years later. *It had become a money-making machine.*

It might not have been the brilliant career I envisioned, but it was definitely a start.

THE GOOD, STEADY JOB…

After thirteen years at The Associates, I took some time off to be with my young children – and of course, do a little more marketing on the side. No chance I was going to give up my passion just because I had a couple of kids…

Ironically, it was one of those kids who led me

Fun 2-step mail sequence we created for a ballroom dance studio.

to my next big move. My daughter was nearing college age, and I decided that if I was going to get another full-time job, I was going to get a job that would not only pay me a salary, but would also pay for my daughter's education. What can I say – I'm a big believer in ROI! Soon, I was back in the corporate world as Procurement Specialist for the University of Notre Dame, making money AND earning a nearly tuition free college education from a top university for my daughter.

3 sequence mailing we did for a student organization for Purdue University. ROI was over 4,000% and they were receiving money more than 4 years later. The white #10 envelope mailing was the 3rd in the sequence and had people begging them to keep sending them mail and telling them they should be in marketing. Done right—#10 envelopes can really work.

Not a bad deal. But again, the job had nothing to do with marketing – unless you count being marketed *to*. As a Procurement Specialist, I was in charge of buying a lot of stuff for the school -- copiers, computers, printing, and promotional items. Everyone wants to sell to Notre Dame, so I saw first-hand just what major corporations were doing to try to get the business of a major university.

And, as a 'Lover of Marketing', I also couldn't help noticing what they *weren't* doing.

I'll never forget the day I received an oversized mail piece from a huge corporation. It was shrink wrapped to protect the beautiful marketing piece inside. I tore it open and read it word for word. No where in that entire piece did it ask for my business or give me a time sensitive offer.

It was all about THEM.

How big THEY were.

How important THEY were.

Contrast that to a letter in a #10 envelope I also got that same day from a chiropractor friend of mine who's a brilliant marketer. I knew instantly 'it would pull response like crazy', but I had to find out how much so I called him. 65% response!!!! He had to quit mailing them they were so overwhelmed with business.

I've learned over the years that there are two kinds of marketing. First, there's institutional marketing – for things like banks and universities and big corporations. That's all about serious concepts like Brand and Image.

But my post-college marketing mentor, Dan Kennedy, taught me about a second kind of marketing I never learned about in college. One where you actually reach out and make a personal connection with the prospect or customer – and really have fun. He introduced me to the world of Direct Response Marketing. Every dollar spent on marketing had to have a measurable response. And at that moment, I knew I truly found my passion.

THE AFFAIR...

I couldn't hold out any longer.

I started cheating occasionally on my Day Job.

Lucky for me, my bosses at Notre Dame knew about my dalliances and let me go ahead with what would become a full-fledged affair.

I started with the university computer store. They had never made more than 300k selling computer equipment to incoming freshmen during the two week back-to-school time. I volunteered to do the two week marketing for the store (under the radar, of course) and that year with just two direct mail pieces tripled their profits to $900,000.

The next year, they wanted more sales while giving me exactly zero dollars to work with. Some people might consider that a disadvantage, but to me, it was more like a challenge. I created a Back-To-School

My Back-to-School newspaper for Notre Dame was a million dollar mailing.

computer store newspaper and sold advertising in it to pay for it. I took all the pictures, wrote all the ads, and did the entire layout. Again – quietly under the radar. That year, the university store made $1.3 million – a full million more than they did before we started working together.

However, possibly my greatest challenge was posed by the school laundry service. "Fun" and "Sexy" aren't words that immediately come to mind when you think of washing your clothes. Now, people love being part of a club, so I created a "Laundry Club" complete with VIP and VIP Gold levels of membership. We sent out the mailer in early July with an "application form" – yes, you had to apply to join our very exclusive Laundry Club – to fax back, sign up for online, or call in to join.

There was such a huge response that the university fax machine ran out of paper, and the laundry's voice mail service was filled with frantic phone calls from would-be Laundry Club VIPS. And, ...the end result? The school laundry service made eighty thousand dollars more than ever before. And I was a bonafide marketing success.

THE HAPPILY EVER AFTER...

My daughter graduated from Notre Dame in May, 2008. And the very next day, I quit my procurement job and devoted myself to my own business –

Audio business cards we produce for clients to hand out to prospects as part of their "shock and awe" package. These are DVD cases with an interview CD and sometimes testimonial booklets inside. We produce for clients. We design the cover and script and produce a 14 minute audio interview

MegaBucks Marketing.

Today, we're doing incredible business all over the world, for clients large and small. And while we may be known as *The Wallet Mailer People* – which, by the way, we don't mind at all! -- that's only been part of the secret to our success.

For me, marketing is all about creativity – about finding that new and different way to make my client stand out from the competition. In an age where all of us are constantly being marketed to, only the outrageous stands out. If 4-color is normal, I do black and white. If big is normal, I do small. If everyone sends #10 envelopes, I mail Frisbees.

And it doesn't stop there. My copy is fun and personal. Whether it's online or offline, there's one thing for certain. …**outrageous personality reigns!**

For me, the fun is in finding the exact right piece of marketing for each and every one of my clients. It's almost like solving a puzzle. And yes, I'll admit a lot of my clients first come to me asking for a wallet mailer. But chances are they'll leave with something completely different… Something perfect… Something that fits them and their target consumer like a glove.

One of my clients had a car repair shop. He'd been in business for 38 years and had the cleanest shop I'd ever been in. I created a simple referral program for him where I wrote a 4-minute script he read and we recorded. I then designed a special $10 business card that on the back told about

Referral CD we created for an auto repair shop.. BEST ROI of any marketing ever done!

the referral program. The CD and ten of the $10 business bills were put into a CD sleeve and propped up with two pieces of candy on the floor between the two front seats - with the headline on the CD that said "Pop This CD in Your CD Player for a Special Message".

He set the first CD on the floor, artfully perched between two Tootsie Rolls… And we waited…

Not long after that customer drove off, he called my client. He told him it was the best marketing idea he'd ever seen. You see, the message from my client on the CD thanked the customer for their business, told them about the referral program and then the top 9 reasons why to do business with his repair shop. All in a span of four minutes.

Ultimately, my client told me the CD Referral Candy Campaign had the best ROI of any campaign ever. People were begging for more of the $10 bills to hand out to their friends and family. *It had 'gone viral'.*

SHARING THE LOVE...

To me, that's what marketing is all about. Making that connection between customer and product or service. And we have all kinds of unique ways of making that connection.

One of our most popular is our magazine "tear sheets" that look exactly like the real thing – with our client on the cover and a great story about their product or service inside. It positions them to be the expert, a celebrity.

We make our clients instantly famous by putting them on one of our 4-page magazine tear sheets. We design the piece and write all the headlines and inside copy. We can even design it with space for 3 ads which the client can sell to pay for the publication. Triple win for everyone. See www.magtearsheets.com

We design and write monthly custom newsletters for clients of all kinds with segments like "Meet the Staff," "Patient of the Month," and, for one dentist, a column "written" by his golden retriever, Bailey. *'Bailey's Blog'* is an especially big hit with the patients.

We design and mint business card coins.

We mail in popcorn bags, manila file folders, and medical pill bottles. We shoot fun client videos. Nothing is off limits when our creative juices get going.

Business Card Coin I designed for a client. 1.75" in diameter and 3mm thick, these never get thrown away.

There's no better way to stay in touch with clients and prospects than through a printed and mailed newsletter. Secret to their success: Don't make them boring and add lots of pictures! Clients hire us to design and write their newsletters.

And we're always ready to come up with something new and different. That's really the most fun of all.

I've kind of gone the long way around to find my true passion. People ask me how I became so successful. It's simple. Like Winston Churchill – I never gave up. I wouldn't be doing what I'm doing today if I did -- I'd be working at some big corporation in a nice office with a big staff. I'm sure I'd be doing an excellent job. But I wouldn't be doing what I love.

And the immortal Churchill words don't just apply to those big decisions, they also apply to the little moments. Great marketing isn't all about one success after another, it's about not being afraid to try new things. If something doesn't work, you can change it, improve it, or save it for another time and try something else. But if it does, you may come up with *the Next Great Idea.*

...And never be known by your real name again.

ABOUT NINA

Nina Hershberger spent 22 years in Corporate America before the entrepreneurial itch grew too strong. As director of a direct mail operation printing and mailing 9 million pieces a month, she naturally gravitated to direct mail when she began her marketing firm. Known world-wide as the wallet mailer lady (for her direct mail piece that looks like a man's paper wallet), it wasn't long before business owners were seeking her out for her outrageous, personality driven marketing advice and her business grew well beyond direct mail. Today she loves making celebrities out of her clients and their pets through her magazine tear sheets and humor copywriting for pets. If you're lucky enough to book some of her scarce time, beware: she just may ask you (or your pet) to don an Elvis Wig and sunglasses and turn you into a personality your prospects and customers can't wait to hear from again.

CHAPTER 12
STAND OUT WITH WEB VIDEO!

by Charlie McDermott,
President, StandOUT Video and Marketing

HOW TO STAND OUT

When you really want to connect with someone, what do you do? You do everything possible to meet them face-to-face. Once you have that kind of personal interaction, there's a much better chance of making a lasting connection and accomplishing what you want with that person – whether it's a business, social, or romantic goal.

When you're a marketer, however, you obviously can't meet in person with every single one of the thousands, or even *hundreds* of thousands of potential customers out there. Door-to-door salesmen went the way of Dictaphones long ago, and you wouldn't want to put in that kind of endless effort even if you could.

So what's the next best thing to making that face-to-face connection? How do you personally pitch yourself and your product?

How do you Stand Out? ......*WITH VIDEO!!!!*

The only reason movie actors become stars is because the public sees them in their roles and *likes* them. Are they more important than the person who wrote the script? Or the director or producer? In the grand scheme of things, they're probably a lot *less* important. That's not easy for me to say, since my son happens to be an actor – but because of the power that comes from *seeing and hearing* performers, they're the element audiences come out to see.

It's the same with news anchors, commercial spokespersons, and reality TV contestants. Whoever is in *front* of the camera gets all the attention. *They Stand Out.* That's why, if you're a marketer or any kind of professional, video can make the difference for your business. I learned that important lesson early on - you need to Stand Out and video is the best vehicle to make that happen.

HOW VIDEO HELPED ME STAND OUT

I began my entrepreneurial journey by owning and running a health club. It did okay, but I was anxious to expand. I finally found a second great location that was available, so I committed to an expensive lease that was actually a stretch for me financially at the time. But, I figured, I had 3 months until the first big rent check was due and I could find a way to make it work.

It was 1990, so nothing involving the Internet was about to do the trick at that point. But I still thought that video could be the key to our success – so we put together our own one-hour TV show featuring group exercise workouts led by my wife. We put it on local cable, I got several local businesses to advertise on it to pay for its production, and, by the end of the 3 month deadline, the club was profitable and I could write that check without sweating it.

I built my health club chain up to 5 locations, before I decided to sell it. I got out of the business because my teenage son, also named Charlie McDermott (he always beats me out in Google searches – I just don't stand a chance), was beginning to get acting roles in small independent movies, and we decided to move him to Hollywood to help his career along. Once again I had a deadline – we would give it six months to see if he could make it. And once again, I decided some marketing magic would help him Stand Out.

This time, I couldn't figure out the way to utilize video, but I did the next best thing – I took out a full-page ad in both "Variety" and "The Hollywood Reporter" to introduce my son to Tinseltown. I did utilize testimonials, however – as my son had just acted in a film with Kris Kristofferson, and Kris generously agreed to give a quote for the ad that said Charlie and Dakota Fanning were two of the best teenage actors that he had ever worked with. It was the kind of quote that would get attention.

That ad prompted a cold call from an agent at the super talent agency, ICM. Casting directors also remembered the ad when Charlie came in for auditions. Today, I'm proud to say he's a regular on the well-received ABC comedy, "The Middle," starring Patricia Heaton from "Everybody Loves Raymond," which is already renewed for next season.

THE VIRTUES OF VIDEO

Once Charlie turned 18, we knew he'd be okay and I moved back home – and started StandOUT Video and Marketing. The basis of my new company was my own personal marketing philosophy – if you don't get noticed, you don't stand a chance. You have to break through the clutter any way you can.

Check out one of my websites, www.GetStandOUT.com, and you'll see exactly how I do that with our videos. We make them creative, fun, and interactive with your site. By using our studio's green screen technology, we can put personalities in any location – or have them "peek out" from behind your own website boxes. As a matter of fact, by visiting my other website, www. StandOUTvideo.com, you'll find an opt-in box that, if you put in your website information, will allow you to see how one of our StandOUT videos could work on your website – instantly!

I use both my business experience and my Hollywood experience to help our clients create videos that deliver their targeted message in an entertaining way. Having spent a lot of time on TV and movie sets for 10 to 15 years, I have a good idea of what works and what doesn't work when presenting your personality, or the personality of whomsoever you choose to represent your business in your videos.

There are several key traits you want to have come across on video – you want to be compelling, trustworthy, and personable, and you want people to be comfortable with you and *like* you. The more they get to know you through your video, the more they'll feel good about buying from you. *As we all know, one of the golden rules of sales is that people buy people.* Video delivers that all-important personal touch.

At the same time, we want to make sure you are getting your marketing message across. So we keep in mind your goal, who you are speaking to, and, at the end of the day, what exactly you want to accomplish. Is this video designed to spur an 'opt-in', a purchase or just present information? Your video has to have a purpose and it should succeed at that purpose.

Whatever your objective, my experience is that using online video completely *works*. For example, I've helped make Jim Palmer, who's known as "The Newsletter Guru," make dozens of videos. Traffic to his site doubled in 30 days once he began using them, and six months later, it's tripled. Another client, an attorney, noticed that visitors to his site were staying 2 to 3 times longer once he began using our videos, which helps his Google search results ranking.

Studies back up these clients' success stories. The Wharton School at the University of Pennsylvania conducted a major study on print vs. video and found that comprehension was 50% higher with video than with straight copy, and that video 'sped-up' buying decisions by 72%. Other studies have shown that video in general increases sales conversions by 30%.

Basically, it's hard to lose when you use video on your website. The worst-case scenario is someone comes to your site and doesn't 'opt in', but they stay longer than they normally would have to watch the video – which, as mentioned earlier, boosts your Google ranking. Best case? Your video helps people to focus in on your message and converts traffic to all-important sales.

HOW WE CREATE YOUR VIDEO

Our process is simple with clients. We start with a phone call to discuss the content of the video. Some clients know exactly what they want to say, but some aren't sure, and we help them develop a script. We then adapt one of our effective, proven formats to help them create their video in our studio at StandOUT, keeping in mind that we want to showcase why they're unique, and help them achieve their ultimate marketing goal. Our client just has to show up to say their lines – because we do everything from there. We incorporate the necessary special effects and we also do the actual placement on our clients' websites.

In a few months, we're going to launch a new and innovative service that will make it even easier for online marketers to add video to their sites. We're going to offer a video membership that will allow you to look at hundreds and hundreds of our stock videos and install them yourself with a click - you'll be able to put as many as you want on your site. In other words, within five minutes, you can go from a site with absolutely no video to a site with lots of video that converts for you better, and keeps visitors at your site longer, to help your Google ranking. Check us out at: www.Snap2Video.com.

And by the way, you don't have to stop with just a short video on your website. There's no better way to really position yourself as an expert than to do your own Web TV show. It worked to sell my health club – and it can work to sell you and your business.

With your own online TV show, you can also sell advertising and create another stream of revenue, or just use it to educate people on your products and services. At our website: www.StandOUT.tv, you'll find more information and specifics about how we can help you set up your own show. Again, we can help you with the entire process from start to finish.

The power of video marketing has impressed even me. My company didn't even exist over a year ago – and we've become incredibly successful in a very short time. Of course, we wouldn't be where we are today without the help of the Glazer-Kennedy Insiders Circle. I'm proud to say that I provided the first video blog ever to DanKennedy.com – and it really helped us make a name for ourselves.

No one has the time or energy to try and make a personal pitch to every potential customer out there. Thanks to online video, you don't have to – the video does it for you. There's no question video has worked wonders for myself and for my clients.

Give it a try so that you, too, can Stand Out.

ABOUT CHARLIE

Charlie McDermott of Stand Out Video & Marketing (GetStandOut.com) is known for his unique use of compelling and entertaining video to dominate Google, generate traffic and increase response. He is a speaker, author, coach, well-known Internet TV personality (StandOut.tv) and the creator of Snap2Video® (Snap2Video.com) the only site on the Internet that Instantly Increases the Power of your Website with Video… In A SNAP!

CHAPTER 13
THROW THE BOOK AT 'EM!

by Nick Nanton, Esq. & J.W. Dicks, Esq.

I entered the huge chain bookstore, hoping my guilty expression wouldn't give me away. Then I furtively disappeared between two large shelves of books in the back, making sure no store employees were looking at me. I eyed the area around me one more time – no one in sight.

And then I pulled the brand new copy of my latest book out from under my jacket…headed to the nearest open cashier…smiled to myself as she scanned the book's ISBN bar…and I paid $21.95 for a book. *A book I already owned.*

My name is Nick Nanton…and I am a reverse shoplifter.

Why am I committing a crime against myself? I'll explain a little later… but first, I want to tell you that this may be one of the most controversial chapters in this book… And not because I'm moving around in bookstores in a clandestine manner.

It's because I'm about to advocate something that I believe delivers one of the biggest ROIs of anything out there today. But it's also something that many people regard as being as dead as the dodo.

What am I talking about?

Well, I'm talking about what you're reading *right this minute.*

A book.

A book can be an amazing platform for your business – it's got prestige, it's got impact and, most importantly, you can market yourself and your business through it in a 'whole bunch' of different ways. Because, to be honest, it doesn't do you any good to write a book and then just put it on your shelf next to that dusty dictionary. It only makes a huge difference when you use your book pro-actively to expand your circle of influence, build your reputation and impress current and prospective clients.

Look at the super-successful people who put out books on a regular basis – people like Donald Trump. He doesn't need to write books to prove himself any more – he can make as much money doing a couple of speeches here and there. No, he – and mega-motivational stars like Tony Robbins and Jack Canfield – create books for the above reasons. It's not about getting paid for the book – it's about growing their brands.

Just look at what happens when "the Donald" writes a book. Suddenly you see him everywhere – Larry King, Fox News, even The View. It gives him a whole new set of talking points and a reason to put himself out there. He knows that the ROI on a book is unlimited – as long as you realize it's not just a book, it's a gigantic marketing tool. That's why it's something I advise all my clients to do.

I'm going to detail in this chapter just how you can make your book go to work for you in a variety of ways. First of all, let's talk about the book itself.

MAKING YOUR BOOK HAPPEN

The first thing you should do is be realistic. You're probably not creating a New York Times Bestseller here – that's not even what you're really after. You make money from *having* a book – not from book sales. This is meant as a marketing tool to sell yourself and your business. Put your book together with that in mind.

As with any marketing tool, you want your book to be an attention-getter. That starts with the title – finding a way to put the concept of the book in a short, 'punchy' and powerful statement that taps into something people want to know.

Simple is very important. Has there ever been a better title than "The Secret?" Well, there haven't been many better-selling titles, anyway. At the same time, it's a gutsy title – because without the multi-million ad campaign for the book, its generic title could have left it lost in the shuffle. Since you're mostly going to be sharing this book with clients and prospects, and not trying to sell it to the general public to a great extent, you can get away with that kind of approach.

Of course, you're thinking, the title is the easy part – what about the content? Well, that might be easier than you think as well. Do you give seminars or create instructional materials? Have you given speeches about your business? That's content – content you had to think about and structure accordingly. By getting these materials transcribed, you could already have the bare bones of your book content.

What happens next depends on your available time and your level of confidence. Let's start with time – most entrepreneurs and business people just don't have enough hours in the day to run their businesses and their lives, let alone try to write a book. It's time-consuming and requires a lot of thought. Many who try it simply give up and don't finish.

Then there's the confidence factor - you may be intimidated by the thought of even trying to write a book. Most people don't even like to write a short blog – and then there are those wouldn't be 'caught dead' even trying to put together the 140 characters or less that go into a "tweet."

That's why most business people will use a ghostwriter to get their book down on paper. You can find excellent ghostwriters on Elance.com (where they'll bid for the chance to work on your book), or you can ask business associates if they've worked with someone they like and trust.

It's easy to work with a ghostwriter – you either give them the kind of transcripts we talked about earlier or you can talk through the main points of the book with them. The important thing is to end up with something that you can feel good about. If you're going to use a book as a marketing platform, you want to make sure it's professional, informational, and represents you and your business in the best possible light.

THE THREE STAGES OF MARKETING YOUR BOOK

Once you have your book finished and published, it's time to *really* go to work. You can maximize your marketing punch not only when your book is published, but also before and after. Again, authoring a book is impressive – so make the most of it!

1. Make Pre-Launch A Priority

You definitely want people to know your book is coming out in advance. Begin by creating a website about the book before it comes out – offer a free portion of the book (a "sneak peek") through an 'opt-in' box that will allow you to capture leads. You can even feature a "countdown" to the publication date and time to generate more excitement.

When the website is up, put out a press release announcing you've got a publishing deal, making sure you have links back to your website. Syndicate the press release and post it on all the social media sites (Facebook, Twitter, etc.). Also consider doing a podcast by having a friend interview you about the book and put it up for download on iTunes.

2. Generate Publication Publicity

Once your book is published, you can now use it to your advantage to get booked just like Donald Trump does. You probably won't make it to "Larry King Live," but you have a 'good shot' at some local air time at the very least.

Next, send out copies of your book to local radio and TV stations, as well as print publications, and offer to be interviewed. Also put in a listing in Radio-TV Interview Report (find out more at RITR.com) to make yourself available for national interviews. You can also mail copies to your top clients, send them out to get yourself booked for speaking engagements at business and civic events, and host a book signing event at a local book store.

You can also continue to produce podcasts for distribution through iTunes with a theme of something like …"Beyond the Book," offering additional/updated information and conversation about topics you cover in the book.

And remember my "reverse shoplifting" at the beginning of this chapter? Here's why you should consider taking a copy of your book into a bookstore

– and buying it there!

As long as your book has a legitimate ISBN number and is available from a major distributor, two things we always do for our clients' books, the bookstore clerk will simply scan the book's barcode, a price will come up and you can purchase it, even though the store never stocked it in the first place. Best of all, the bookstore's computer system will register that somebody bought your book and that they're now out of stock – meaning they just might order more copies of your book to sell on their own!

3. Create A Long Afterlife

Now that you're an author, it should become an important part of your professional profile. Make sure it's added to your official bio and possibly even put the name of the book in your email signature for a limited time.

You can also break down a chapter and make it into a free 'special report', available on your website through an 'opt-in' box. Other chapters can be turned into online articles that you can syndicate, or you can rework the material into speeches or seminar material for your personal or recorded appearances.

Your office should also reflect your author status. Put a framed copy of the cover of your book on the wall in your reception area or office – it's easy to do through canvaspop.com. Also, leave copies of your book on the coffee table in your office with "Take Me" stickers on the front. You should also donate copies to the local libraries in your area. Make sure your contact information is contained in these copies – either put a business card in the book, or have your info stamped on the back page.

At our Celebrity Branding Agency®, we take this process through another, very powerful step. We've created a foolproof way to make our authors' books best-sellers in certain Amazon categories. We then honor them by placing them in our National Academy of Best-Selling Authors™ - and send out another round of press releases noting their honor and best-selling status, which opens up a whole world of marketing opportunities for the same book.

They say print is dead, but, thanks to Kindle, iPad and other electronic devices, it's not really. It's just migrated to LCD screens. The fact is that nothing conveys authority and credibility more than having a published book with your name on it. Publishing a book and marketing it correctly puts you and your business up more than 'a few notches' against the competition – and isn't that what it's all about?

And, best of all….reverse shoplifting is NOT against the law!

ABOUT J.W.

J.W. Dicks, Esq. is America's foremost authority on Personal Branding for Business Development. He has developed some of the most successful mass media and multi-channel business marketing campaigns in the country and built multi-million dollar businesses on the back of them – to the tune of more than $500,000,000 in sales.

J.W. represents some of the top marketers and professional experts in the world in the growth of their businesses using online and offline business development systems, social media, multi-dimensional marketing, franchising and strategic legal structure to accomplish their goals and capitalize on the assets they create.

A Best-Selling author with more than 14 published books, and hundreds of articles, J.W. has also been quoted or appeared in Newsweek, The Wall street Journal, USA Today, NBC, ABC, CBS, and FOX affiliates as well as Entrepreneur's Start-Up Magazine, Forbes.com, CNN.com, and many other national and local media outlets.

In addition to coaching and consulting for clients nationwide, J.W. is also a successful entrepreneur living in the trenches himself. He has built his own businesses, with annual sales exceeding $35 Million, developed real estate in excess of $200 Million and created and sold intellectual property rights for as much as $1.8 Million.

Jack is a graduate of the University of Florida and George Mason College of Law. He is a member of the American Bar Association, NASD, National Association of Realtors, the Florida Bar and the Virginia Bar.

Jack's business address is in Orlando, and his play address is at his beach house where he spends as much time as he can with his wife of 37 years, Linda, and their two Yorkies. His major hobby is fishing… although the fish are rumored to be safe.

Jack can be reached at JWDicks@DicksNanton.com

ABOUT NICK

Nick Nanton, Esq. is known as "The Celebrity Lawyer" for his role in developing and marketing business and professional experts into Celebrity Experts in their field, through personal branding, to help them gain credibility and recognition for their accomplishments. Nick is recognized as the nation's leading expert on personal branding as Fast Company Magazine's Expert Blogger on the subject and lectures regularly on the topic at the University of Central Florida. His book Celebrity Branding You® has been selected as the textbook on personal branding at the University.

Nick serves as the Producer of America's PremierExperts® television show and The Next Big Thing® radio show, both designed to recognize the top Experts in their field and bring their solutions to consumers.

Nick is an award winning songwriter, television producer and, the co-author of the best-selling books, Celebrity Branding You!®, Big Ideas for Your Business and Shift Happens. Nick also serves as editor and publisher of Celebrity Press™, a publishing company that produces and releases books by top Business Experts. Nick has been featured in USA Today, The Wall St. Journal, Newsweek, The New York Times, Entrepreneur® Magazine, FastCompany.com and has appeared on ABC, NBC, CBS, and FOX television affiliates speaking on subjects ranging from branding, marketing and law, to American Idol.

Nick is a member of the Florida Bar, holds a JD from the University of Florida Levin College of Law, as well as a BSBA in Finance from the University of Florida's prestigious Warrington College of Business. Nick is also a voting member of The National Academy of Recording Arts & Sciences (NARAS, Home to The GRAMMYs) and spends his spare time working with Young Life, Florida Hospital and rooting for the Florida Gators with his wife Kristina, and their two sons, Brock and Bowen.

Nick can be reached at Nick@CelebrityBrandingAgency.com

CHAPTER 14
PROFITING FROM PERFORMANCE

by Dustin Mathews, A.J. Puedan & Dave VanHoose,
The Speaker's Dream Team

A great performance can move you, touch you and amaze you. A great performance makes you totally believe in the actor's reality – and keeps you captivated throughout a film or TV show. The right personality with the right script hooks you and keeps you watching until the end credits. *You never forget a great performance.*

If you just read the script they made the movie from, however, it would be a completely different experience. Yeah, you would probably like it. But when the right actor 'breathes creative fire into it', its power is magnified to the 'nth' degree. Suddenly, you're bonding with a real person, you're investing yourself personally in what's going to happen next – and, when the satisfying pay-off happens, you ride an emotional high out of the theatre.

Now, let's exit Hollywood and talk about marketing your business. Specifically, let's talk about *your* potential great performance – the one that, instead of winning you an Oscar, could make you a fortune.

For entrepreneurs, online landing pages, flyers, emails, direct mail and the like are all effective selling tools. But they're also kind of like reading the movie script instead of seeing the movie. They're just words and images on a paper or on a screen. The product or service may be awesome, but if there's no personality behind it, the sale may not be as easy as you planned.

That's why all across America, all across the world, entrepreneurs make it a point to present their own products and services in webinars and online videos, as well as speak at seminars, conferences and other events, so they can sell who they are and what their business is *with their own personality*. They know that making that personal connection is all-important in expanding their brand and developing ongoing relationships with customers and prospects.

Yes, they're smart about all that. The problem, though, to be blunt…is that most of them are doing it *completely wrong*.

THE SPEAKER'S DREAM TEAM

The three of us have attended countless seminars and sales events in our careers, and together, we have a combined 24 years of experience in this arena. Dave, in particular, used to give a sales pitch twice a day, five days a week for three years – over 500 presentations a year - and he learned firsthand what works and what doesn't work simply through pure experience. All of us have watched countless speakers doing a wide variety of different pitches and presentations and made it a practice of analyzing how well they accomplished their goals with their talks.

When we sat down and compared notes, even though we came from three very different experience bases, we agreed that only *about 5% of speakers we saw actually knew what they were doing*. That's a pretty high fail rate. And it comes from the fact that most of these speakers just didn't put the time into crafting an effective presentation – or just plain didn't have the knowledge or training to do it correctly. Even the ones who were actually selling effectively had no idea why their talks were working.

We spoke to many of them and asked why they did their presentations the way they did them. It turns out most of them were flying blind, just putting their talks together without a thought to a solid sales structure and without really researching what makes a talk *sell*.

To the three of us, this discovery was mind-boggling. What's the point in addressing people directly in whatever format if you're not going to make it count? Obviously, there was an opportunity for us to help speakers deliver to an audience in a foolproof way. So, in 2009, we began – and became - "The Speaker's Dream Team."

The first thing we did, based again on our extensive experience, was to perfect the most persuasive presentation format on the planet. This formula for sales success was designed to help any client close the deal with his speech. And it proved to be a potent tool.

Our award-winning services helped us train 400 people in our first year of business. Many of them ended up making millions in the six months after utilizing our services. One woman, who had been in business for less than a year, recently did $400,000 in sales in one boot camp weekend after working with us.

We don't relate these success stories to brag – we tell them because we want speakers to know how huge an ROI they can obtain just from using our secret formula that we're going to share a little later in this chapter (yes, folks, we've giving it all away – it's your lucky day!). Our clients spend anywhere from $10,000 to $25,000 a day for our training, because they know it's going to pay off for them in many multiples of those fees.

We do it *all* for our clients, except actually getting up there and talking for them. We help them write their scripts, work on their Powerpoints, we record them doing their presentation, review it with them, and rerecord it until it works. It's no different than Morgan Freeman or Meryl Streep preparing to do the kind of great performance like we discussed at the beginning of this chapter. Those A-list actors first get an awesome script, then they memorize their lines and finally, they work on their actual *acting* – the equivalent of our coaching our clients when they perform.

But it all starts with the script. And that's where our formula comes in. If you follow our formula, you've got a good shot at success. If you don't…well, you're 'shooting in the dark'. And that always means you might just hit your own foot.

THE TOP TEN IMPORTANT STRATEGIES FOR ANY SALES PRESENTATION

These ten strategies will guide you from the beginning to end of whatever your sales pitch is all about. Follow them and success will follow you.

1. **Grab people's attention when you get onstage.** *The first 7 seconds of your talk are the most important.* That's when people decide whether they like you – or the unpleasant other option. Get your audience into a "yes" state if you can, by asking questions they will automatically answer "yes" to (example: "Does anyone here want to make money?" Odds favor a positive response!) If you can get an audience to say "yes" at least 7 times during your presentation, you have an awesome shot at closing deals.

2. **Tell them what you're going to tell them.** It helps them to concentrate on your message and wonder how you're going to deliver on your initial promises.

3. **Have a sales outcome in mind.** This may sound ridiculous, but many speakers get up to talk – and have *absolutely nothing* to sell! *Make sure you always have an outcome in mind.* Are you selling your website? A product? Your brand? Whatever your outcome is, let the audience know about the opportunity you're offering them right away. Once they know what you're trying to pitch them, the tension around what you're doing up there vanishes – and that's a good thing, because you can then concentrate on actually doing 'the sell'. Example – you get up there and say you have a complete real estate foreclosure system, all done for you, for a $12,000 investment. Your audience will then participate in your speech to validate your system – is it worth the cost? Does it really work? People aren't stupid – so allow them to participate in your pitch, rather than playing cute.

4. **Stories sell, facts tell.** *If you're just listing statistics and facts, you're*

not really emotionally connecting with your audience. Let's go back to our acting example. Imagine Tom Cruise just saying "I'm very worried because there are five people shooting at me," instead of actually relating to the situation with his performance. Wouldn't work too well. People learn from stories and connect to them – it helps you build rapport at a deeper level. Ideally, your stories offer dramatic turning points where your product or service turns around people's lives – rags-to-riches stories are especially potent. As a side note, don't put too many words on your Powerpoint slides – keep them simple so the audience is looking at you and not reading what's on your slides. Make sure, however, to brand each of your slides with the name of your company or product in a consistent place.

5. **Use testimonials as social proof.** *People want to make sure your product or service does the job it's supposed to.* Having a lot of testimonials with names and photos or video attached are real evidence to your audience that what you're selling *works.* People get excited by them – if other people can find success with what you're selling, then they realize they can do it too. It's a crucial factor to overcoming sales resistance.

6. **Give the benefit.** Let's be real. Your audience isn't there to buy your product or service. They're there to buy what it can do for them – *the benefit.* All buying systems are based on emotions – that's why stories and testimonials bring "people power" to your presentation. <u>*You have to tell them what's in it for them.*</u> Whether it saves them time, builds their business, gives them financial freedom, whatever…make sure you sell the benefit in a compelling way. Take them from pain to pleasure – elaborate on the pain they're experiencing now in their lives and embellish on the pleasure they'll obtain from your product.

7. **Make trial closes *throughout* your presentation.** Most people think they just need to do a close at the end of their talk. Wrong. Remember what we said about the "yes" state in our number 1 strategy? *Continue to ask questions that your audience will say "yes" to throughout your entire speech – that relate directly back to your product or service.* Questions like, "How many of you understand that this will change your life?" "Who here wants to double their income?" etc. Small commitments lead to big commitments. And as you ask these questions, anchor your product to these positive-answer questions. Touch or hold up the product when you ask them – let the audience feel the physical connection between the benefit you're bringing up and the product you're selling. If you want people to go to a table in the back of the room to make the purchase after your talk, point to that table during your talk.

8. **Make actual value a part of your actual close.** As you wind up your speech, break down the specific values of parts of your product. "This webinar is worth $345, this course book is worth $298," etc., so the

audience sees they're getting an incredible value. *And drop the price down during your final close.* Yes, everyone expects it – *but it works.* And, finally give them a compelling Call to Action to motivate them to buy. Use the law of scarcity to your advantage – the first ten people who buy get 20% off, etc. Also offer a lot of bonuses – a free coaching call, two tickets to your boot camp, whatever. Bonuses that don't cost you anything but give you another chance to market to them are ideal. You will also be able to obtain bonuses from other speakers and experts who would love a shot at marketing to your group – they'll probably be willing to give you an affiliate deal so that if someone buys from them, you get a cut.

9. **Offer a guarantee.** Again, this seems like a no-brainer, but it's something you have to have in place. *The number one reason someone will not buy what you're selling is because they have been ripped off before by a similar product.* That's why the guarantee is VERY important. Either a 7 day money back guarantee or something similar of your choosing – where the customer feels like they have some control over getting back their money if the product doesn't work for them.

10. **Do "The Free Close."** Finally, *offer a way for your audience to get the product for free.* It could be a trial offer, it could be some kind of partnership venture with you, whatever. Find a way to make it happen.

Now that we've given away many of our secrets, let's throw in a few more as *your* bonus (we have to practice what we preach, right?). So, very briefly, let's discuss the importance of both pre-selling yourself before the event you're appearing at, and following up with the new contacts you made as a result of your presentation.

When it comes to the pre-sale, we make sure each of our clients is positioned correctly before they open their mouths. Most speakers don't know how to market themselves – we provide them with a marketing kit, advance emails and a bunch of other "preliminary events" that organizers can use to advertise you and your speech. These things help to establish you as a guru and enhance your credibility. When you're seen as the expert, people listen to you – and more importantly, buy from you.

The other critical phase is *after* you've given your talk. You need to collect as many contacts as possible at your talk, by using an incentive such as a free newsletter or other no-cost information - and then you need to follow up with those contacts through email, your sales rep, a sales letter, a phone call – whatever your system is. Many times, *you will get more sales with the follow-up than with the actual talk.* So if you don't do the follow-up, you're leaving money on the table.

How do we know our sales system works? Because we've seen it in action too many times to question it. For example, a national speaker had us analyze his presentation – we fine tuned some things. But he wanted us to try and resell his product for him instead of him doing it himself. Within one day, Dave was up on stage doing the pitch, not really knowing the guy's product or presentation all that well, and, again, he effectively closed sales – because he knows how the formula works.

Another example. Someone who was a great promoter in his own right launched a new social media product to 1400 people on his list. He only sold 29 units – so, naturally he wasn't very happy. He came to us and we reworked his presentation and had him rerecord his webinar. He sent it out again – *to the same list* – and tripled his sales. Now, many of his best customers had already watched it the first time so they skipped it the second. Imagine what the conversion rate would have been if his best customers had taken another look?

We can sell any product with our strategy within 24 hours of getting to know it. We've made millions for others – and our sales strategy can make millions for you. Try out our tips for yourself – or let us coach you to even greater success with our proven tricks and techniques.

We know you've got a great performance in you. Give us the opportunity and we'll make sure the whole world sees it – and more importantly, *buys* it.

ABOUT AJ

They call him "Yoda" because when it comes to the seminar business, no one knows more than AJ. With over 23 years experience (he started at 14) he's secretly pulling out more dollars per head in the industry. Ask him about his $8,750 per head event.

And if you think you have to have a lot of people in your database to make some serious money, just ask AJ how he pulled in $943,000 Dollars with just 300 customers in his database. He's the seminar industry's Best Kept Secret.

ABOUT DAVE

Not only is Dave the leading closer in the country, averaging over $1,000 per head (to free crowds), he's also the coach behind many of the nation's top speakers and closers.

Dave has generated over $14 million in one year in the seminar business. He's also the only guy on the planet 'ballsy' enough to give a presentation only having a day to prepare...and actually closing sales from stage.

ABOUT DUSTIN

Behind every powerful speaker, there is an incredibly powerful marketer. Don't let his boyish looks fool you – he was responsible for filling two hundred events per month which enabled Dave's company to land at No. 35 on the Inc. 500 Fastest Growing Companies.

In the last year he's worked on 9 online product launches creating over $10 million dollars in sales. Now he's creating an automated money machine that will generate over a million in sales with just one part time employee.

CHAPTER 15
EXPECT REFERRALS: THE WHAM OF "WOM"

by Jody Murphy, The Referral Coach

One day, you receive a flyer in the mail for a new hair salon. It tells you how wonderful the place is and invites you to make an appointment.

The next day, you receive an email from a friend. They tried that new hair salon and thought it was amazing – they did a wonderful color and cut and the service was incredible. And you can get a special discount if you give them a try.

Which would make you actually make an appointment at the hair salon?

The answer is fairly obvious. Most people, when they received the flyer, would probably ignore it and throw it in the recycling. Why? Because hair's much too important to put in the hands of people you don't know!

But when someone you know and trust calls you and raves about the same place? Incredibly powerful – because your friend has no ulterior motive in recommending the salon except for the fact that she *wanted you to know how great it was.*

On the other hand, the flyer is an impersonal advertisement that the salon bought and paid for themselves. Just like the other 50 million marketing messages we're bombarded with on a daily basis.

I don't have anything against those kind of marketing messages – it's where I started, doing political direct mail, and they obviously have their place and power in the scheme of things. It used to be fun trying to create the perfect direct mail piece that would make the recipient actually pay attention to our messages!

The plain and simple fact, however, is that when it comes to getting an incredible ROI on a campaign, WOM – Word of Mouth - is definitely one of the most powerful tools a marketer has at their disposal. It's also, however, one of the most difficult tools to implement and exert any control over.

WOM can make or break the biggest Hollywood blockbusters or the smallest local business. If it's good, it's hard not to be a success. If it's bad, it's incredibly hard to overcome and could shut you down for good. That's why it's always vital to get WOM on your side – so we worked hard to create an easy-to-use automatic system to do just that.

CREATING EXPECT REFERRALS

My business partner, Chuck Barnett, and I have been working together for about nine years. We decided our initial focus would be on personalized direct marketing – because we saw the beginning of a shift away from mass mailings and wanted to be ahead of the curve. A year or two ago, we felt another shift beginning, with the rise of Facebook and Twitter – now direct marketing had to be more personalized and targeted in order to be effective. It wasn't enough to just have specific images and names relevant to the recipient in the marketing pieces – they actually wanted to hear from a friend and get a personal recommendation or they didn't think it was credible.

At the same time, the recession hit with a vengeance and suddenly people didn't have the budget to do big direct mail campaigns. And again, in the flood of so many communication messages, those direct mail campaigns didn't seem to be doing a great job on the ROI front. The time was right to start re-educating people on how to use a referral program that was effective. For us, that started with a system that had a lot of built-in value to it.

Our challenge was to create a system that worked with any grassroots referral program, that was as personal as possible – as affordable as possible – and as automatic as possible – to enable small businesses to do social networking on their own platform under *their* control.

As a technology-based marketing company, we decided to build an online turn-key automated system called Expect Referrals that would allow businesses to easily and consistently enable customers to share their good experiences with their friends – and be rewarded for those referrals at the same time. Expect Referrals, which is based at expectreferrals.com, will debut in early summer 2010 and has exceeded our wildest expectations in terms of how effective it is for *our* customers.

HOW EXPECT REFERRALS WORKS

Expect Referrals was created to be a completely automated program that any small business can use with ease. And it works both as a WOM device and a lead generator. We'll get into all that a little later – but first, here's a step-by-step look at how you work with Expect Referrals.

You begin by customizing your own Expect Referrals page template that we provide – you can link to it from your own business website. We provide images you can use, unless you prefer to use your own, and you can either write your own welcome message to customers and referrals, or we can write it for you. The screenshot below will give you more of an idea of the process:

When your customers visit your Expect Referrals page, through the link from your website, they will be taken to this welcome page. They can then click through to our Customer Information Page, shown in the next screenshot, where they can then input their name and contact information. You can also add up to 4 survey questions that you get to determine, if you want to collect more information on your customer base. All that information is stored in the Expect Referrals database.

Once your customer is done with this one-time-only form, they begin providing referrals to your business by filling in the referral contact information. They must provide their friend's name and email address, but they can also provide additional information about themselves to help you get to know them better. They can track whom they sent referrals to and whether or not their friends opened their emails. Plus, they can write a personal message to their friend if they wish that will be included as part of the email.

The referral then gets a personal email – from their friend's email address – featuring the incentive and their friend's personal recommendation, as in the next screen shot.

And finally, when your customer has logged in the necessary number of referrals on your Expect Referrals webpage, they receive their own incentive from your business to keep them continuing to work for you!

Not only are you spreading great WOM on your business, but you're also collecting incredibly valuable customer data, which you can access with a keystroke from your Expect Referrals webpage (as you can see in the next screenshot). You can also download the contact info for every customer and referral whenever you want - PLUS check out a slew of other statistics that help you make your referral program the best it can be.

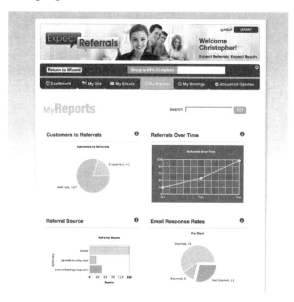

And to make this process even easier, you can even track and redeem the Expect Referrals incentive coupons through the website as well!

HOW EXPECT REFERRALS DELIVERS KILLER ROI

Why do we consider Expect Referrals to be superior to most other referral programs?

Well, I started this chapter out by talking about hair salons, so let me cite another one as an example. This particular hair salon gives you little business card-sized coupons with a discount coupon to give to your friends if they come in for a hair appointment. A friend of mine gave out these cards/coupons to ten different friends – and the hair salon was incredibly excited, because two of the ten people actually came in.

We have a slightly different perspective on that marketing. At Expect Referrals, we look at that not as two successes - but *eight missed opportunities*.

Why? Because if that customer had simply input those ten referrals on the Expect Referrals webpage, instead of handing out cards, that hair salon would have the contact information for *each* of those ten referrals, instead of for only the two who actually came into the salon. And remember, the customer is motivated to provide that information, because if they do, they get their own reward or incentive from the business that they already patronize.

And *that's* why Expect Referrals is a great lead generation tool, as well as being an incredible WOM system. Your customers are actually doing your

114

marketing for you, by delivering valuable quality leads who have a high likelihood of being interested in your product or service. Basically, it's a win-win for everybody. Your customer and the referrals they provide all get a special deal, and you get more potential business and a ton of golden marketing contact info.

Best of all, the whole process is *completely* automated once you customize your Expect Referrals web page and provide the specific incentives. As Richard stressed in the opening chapters of this book, it's incredibly important that a business be able to automatically collect marketing data. Expect Referrals does just that – and creates its own mini-network of customers and referrals that's far more effective than just using Twitter and Facebook to blanket your friends with specials.

This is a *pro-active* system that customers will want to utilize. They already like your business, or they wouldn't be referring it to friends. And because they're return customers, they're going to want the discounts and specials you offer them in exchange for participating on Expect Referrals.

And, by the way, Expect Referrals is especially powerful with businesses that are customer-centric and have already existing programs in place to make sure their customers are happy and satisfied. If your referral program is ever *not* performing the way you want it to, stop and ask yourself … are my current customers happy enough with me to want to share their experience with their friends and family? If not, we should probably talk.

Expect Referrals is also a marketing tool you can use in conjunction with Richard's ROI services. You can add one of Richard's toll-free tracking numbers to different incentives so you can compare how well individual ones work, or use his "Bridge" software package to optimize your conversion rates on the referrals who call for more information and further automate future marketing campaigns.

So yes, we agree that using social media is incredibly important now. But we also think having and controlling your own platform for it, such as the one Expect Referrals provides, is the most effective way to use that kind of online networking. While everyone's blasting their status on Facebook, you're quietly generating new business and leads without breaking a sweat.

And that is what the Wham of "WOM" is all about.

ABOUT JODY

Jody Murphy has been helping clients conduct effective direct marketing campaigns for the past 17 years. From pressure sensitive labels to automated multi-touch programs, Jody has touched on it all, and as a result, she is the arbiter of taste when it comes to copy, art, creative and layout. Jody has handled all types of work including political campaigns for hundreds of candidates, non-profit donor programs, , as well as handling other notable business clients including Walt Disney World, Strang Communications, Natural Awakenings Magazine, Southeast Toyota Distributors and Universal Orlando Resort.

Having worked on thousands of direct marketing campaigns over her career, in the last few years she has become an expert in helping small businesses reach their potential and have a competitive advantage. She does this by creating turn-key tools for them to use to grow their business. "My passion is to make marketing and business development easy for business owners so they can spend less time working on their business and more time doing what they are passionate about. That is why they got into their business in the first place." As one of the founding inventors of ireferTM, a completely automated and personal online referral marketing and lead generation tool, Jody is rewriting the book on how small businesses get to be successful. The easy, affordable and manageable way!

CHAPTER 16
REPETITION IS RECOGNITION

by Jason Ross, CEO and Founder, TSM Studio
and Xcell Advertising

L et's talk boring.

You're sitting in a doctor's waiting room. You're standing in line at the bank. You're waiting for your car to get cleaned at the car wash. We all go through that kind of thing, right? You want to get something done and you have to 'hang out' until it's your turn. Every second seems like an hour, you have absolutely nothing to do, maybe you fool around with your iPhone a little, and that's all you got. You sit – or stand - and you wait.

Well, a while back, there I was in one of those situations, waiting in line at the movies for popcorn. Same kind of deal – there was about to be another three minutes gone from my life.

But then - because I run a multimedia company – I started thinking about how many of the short ads we produced I could be watching while I was standing there in line. At least it would give me something to look at.

And then I thought…Why don't we put ads in locations where these kinds of situations happen? Not just any ads – ads that are cool to look at and entertaining. What could be better than fun, low cost advertising where your potential customers really have nothing better to do than watch commercials and other announcements?

Suddenly, I was glad I got that bored. Because I now was given the gift of a new business.

BORN TO BE AN ENTREPRENEUR

Let me back up a little and talk about how and why I got to the point where I would have that thought and put it into immediate action.

I grew up in Cincinnati, Ohio, where my dad worked his way all the way to the top at a steel fabrication company and became president. Wow, I thought that was pretty cool, my dad was the president of a company! It made me want to run a company when I got older. But what was really awesome about my dad - something I didn't appreciate as much at the time - was that he developed his own side business, one he owned and controlled, that made money from the steel fabricating operation that he ran.

In other words, he used his one business to leverage another completely different business that he could make all the money from.

I guess I was born with his entrepreneurial spirit, because I used his example to build businesses 'from the get-go'. When I was 17, I used to sell car audio products for an independent dealer. He would give me the products to sell, no cost (due to our good relationship), and I would pay him back when I made the sale, keeping a commission for myself, of course.

Well, I was in with a circle of guys who loved to work on cars. And one day, when I had sold a bunch of stereos, I didn't go right back with the money to my supplier. Instead, I drove to Cleveland and bought a gold plating machine. I then lined up three jobs to do some gold plating on emblems for my friend's cars once I had that machine – and suddenly I had enough to pay the guy back for the products as well as pay for the price of the gold plating machine.

One business gets you to another – when you're a true entrepreneur.

I tried to carry that philosophy into my first job after school, working at a music studio about 6 years ago. I saw the internet rising into a real marketing force and figured there were a lot of ways to make money for the studio and not just from music recording - but for online marketing of our clients and so on. The owner was not open to my ideas – he didn't get that 'one business took you to another'. All he wanted to do with the studio was record bands and singers.

So, with no money and no real resources, I decided to begin my own studio – TSM (Trusun Media). From that humble beginning, we've grown and grown – billing over 2 million in service-based business, growing my staff from two to ten people, and working with such celebrities as John Walsh, host of "America's Most Wanted," Orlando Magic star Dwight Howard, "Rush Hour" movie star Chris Tucker, pop singer Gwen Stefani, and many other high profile clients.

It was great to build TSM from the ground up, but I wasn't about to stop there. Being an entrepreneur means you see yourself as a thought machine - your brain never stops wanting to have new ideas and start new ventures. I built TSM not just so I could run my own multimedia company, but also so that I could leverage it to build other businesses that would work with it.

So, yeah, you could say that the night when I was waiting for my movie snacks, I had a lot of stuff already working in the back of my mind that led me to my breakthrough moment.

XCELL ADS

Excited by my new idea, I began a new business named Xcell Media Enterprises, and I went out to several local businesses – including the movie theatre – that would allow me to place screens where I knew there would be a "captive audience" – where, again, people would be in a place where they might be bored and could actually appreciate having something to watch.

I then went to potential clients who might want to advertise in these kinds of locations. It was an easy pitch – because the ROI from this kind of marketing is incredible.

Think about it. If you're used to advertising only in newspapers, local magazines, or coupon books, you have to recognize that this is a dying business. Most people are now getting their news and information online from their Blackberries or laptops. And limiting your business marketing to a daily or weekly paper stops you from reaching a substantial part of your customer base – the core newspaper readership represents less than a third of the entire population.

Same with a magazine. You pay $500 or so for a quarter panel, and someone could easily just turn the page right by it, never to return. Again, how many people don't even read that particular magazine?

Then there are billboards. They're great and people might take a look if they're not actually watching the road like they should be. But the expense is very high – thousands of dollars for a drive-by.

Probably the closest thing to what we do is running commercials on TV. Here, again, a major problem is the huge expense – and the fact that, when the commercial break comes on, people immediately switch channels, make a sandwich or take a bathroom break. Now, add into that mix the relatively new DVR technology that allows most people to just fast-forward through the commercials and you have to admit – TV viewers have got an amazing menu of options when it comes to finding ways to not to watch your ad.

Through our Xcell Advertising Citycast program, however, your ad is repeated in a looped sequence with other commercials in whatever locations you want. We can also easily change those locations and that sequence, as we program all the screen locations from our facility

And again, since your potential customers are "trapped" in a line or a room for several minutes with nothing to do, odds are they will see your ad repeatedly. They say time is money? Well, their time is your money. Not only that, they have no control over the playing sequence – there's no DVR to enable them to skip past something - and, since they have to be where they are to get whatever service they're waiting for, they're not about to leave the room.

The title of this chapter is "Repetition is Recognition" because that's our motto and the key to the power of Xcell Advertising. If someone sees your ad a few times at the same place, then sees your ad repeatedly at another one of our screen locations – they get to know your business pretty quickly – and you become "top of mind" in your business sector.

We had one university advertise with us and not even list their phone number or website – they just wanted to establish their brand with the viewers, and did so successfully. On the other hand, some small businesses may already have their name out there – and, by producing a skillfully-produced and visible Xcell ad, they can convince a consumer that they are a viable company worth giving a try.

Our ads may be on the walls of the businesses where our screens are located, but our concept is incredibly "off-the-wall" compared to traditional media – Xcell brings you very affordable, widespread exposure of your business, where you're guaranteed to get a sizeable audience.

Again, when you watch TV, you get up and do things to avoid the commercial breaks, right? With Xcell Ad Screens, people are exposed to our commercials where they're doing things. It's a part of the overall environment of the kinds of businesses everyone frequents on a daily basis– and the ads can't help but get noticed.

EXPANDING XCELL

Because I do believe one business gets you to another, we've found additional ways to expand the Xcell concept. For brick-and-mortar businesses like medical practices, banks, universities and other locations where there is a lot of traffic, we place screens in waiting areas and provide informational videos.

Now I'm sure you're aware this is already done in some doctor's waiting rooms. For the most part, however, you're just watching an old video with generic content relevant to the doctor's practice and usually some national sponsorship attached.

We take this concept about 100 steps further – by, first of all, personalizing the content about the particular business or practice that the screen is located in. We'll create video that profiles the staff, informs about additional available services, and makes the viewer aware that the receptionist can provide them with a drink of water or a magazine if they want and so on. We call this an "Intracast" – because it's more of a personal experience for the viewer and the business as well – and permits a low-key sale of everything the business has to offer.

Not only that, but we make sure the quality is cutting-edge and as incredible as possible. We provide HD video quality on a Blu-Ray disc – so nobody is stuck watching a fuzzy VHS tape any longer.

A new package we're just now beginning to offer is Point of Sale (POS) Marketing – a small screen that's activated by motion sensors as a customer approaches your cash register. A short ad comes on and suggests a final additional sale – for example, maybe a tempting sweet treat for someone buying groceries. This kind of suggestive selling can make a big difference right where it counts the most – at the place where people pay. POS can also be sponsored by a local business … imagine everyone that goes to check out at a store sees your ad when they do!

Another bonus for our clients is that the videos we produce for them are high-quality, both in terms of production and in creativity. We provide full 3-D animation and fully produced commercials that can compete with the big boys – and we make sure there's enough "eye candy" in them to get a potential customer's attention.

Not only that, but, since our clients have already paid to have their commercials produced, we make sure they can use that existing resource every which way they can. We work with them to place the highly-produced ads online – and use them in social media marketing, by posting them on YouTube, Facebook, etc. and then Twittering links to the videos to do some additional viral marketing.

Finally, we've recently become a partner with the National Center for Missing and Exploited Children (at: www.ncmec.org) so we can help this important cause. Callahan Walsh, John Walsh's son, became a partner last year, because we have been friends for a while and were doing different business ventures together. It was the next logical step to create the Child Recovery Network to display missing children information across the Xcell network. We also allow our clients to sponsor missing children if they want to help the effort. Contributing what we can is a way to give back to the community and make this more than just "business as usual."

We think advertising the Xcell way gives businesses an incredible ROI on their marketing costs. After we produce their commercials for a very affordable one time fee (after that, it's theirs to do with what they want), our clients find it's incredibly cheap to continue to expand the number of Xcell locations their ads are seen on – as well as extend the number of months they run the ads with our screen network. And the business they get as a result of Xcell exposure more than pays for the low cost of placement.

We also offer Richard "The ROI Guy" Seppala's call-tracking systems so our clients can see just how many leads their Xcell ads are generating and which campaigns are most effective. We want to make sure they know we're delivering what we promise.

Xcell will continue to work with the latest technology to serve our clients – currently, we are offering our clients software that will enable them to change their own advertising from their own PCs and laptops. And our fair pricing policies, along with our innovative screen placements, strategies and high production standards, will continue to deliver an incredible value to them.

So, the next time you're bored and waiting in line for something, remember that an amazing business idea could hit you at any moment.

Or better yet, just relax and enjoy the entertaining Xcell ad playing on the screen on the wall in front of you.

ABOUT JASON

Cincinnati born Jason Ross embodies the word entrepreneur in its purest form. At the age of 33 he has created and managed several companies. With his background in entertainment and creative marketing he has fathered the likes of The Bottlestar, a unique bar product; Xcell Advertising, a digital advertising company; and the reputable media powerhouse, Trusun Media (TSM). He has owned and managed a facility and numerous employees for over 6 years and has brought profit to all of his endeavors thus far.

Jason has worked with many high profile clients in audio / video production, and marketing through TSM, such as NBA All-Star Dwight Howard. Grammy Award winning gospel singer, Fred Hammond; Comedian, Chris Tucker, Television Star John Walsh and many more. He has also rendered his expertise in creative marketing and product branding for clients in the entertainment industry and corporate business.

CHAPTER 17
THE FORTUNE AT YOUR FEET

by Ed O'Keefe, Founder, Dentist Profits

Nothing teaches you how to fight for market share like growing up in a big family.

As the 12th of 13 children, I had to develop what it takes to stand out from the crowd (the crowd being my siblings!). When you have that many kids screaming for attention, and you're near the back of the line like I was, you innately develop strategies to compete – and you keep trying new and progressively more creative ones until you discover what works the best.

And maybe that's part of what's helped me do what I do for dentistry practices.

There are, of course, a lot of good dentists out there and all of them want more business. What ends up being the big difference? *Marketing.* By utilizing innovative ways to retain patients, attract new ones and find the right profitable niche, you can easily take an also-ran practice and boost it to superstar status.

That's where I come in. Most dentists, and other professionals like them, benefit from an outside voice to help them develop ongoing techniques to generate leads, upsell existing customers, and grow their practice beyond their normal numbers. Most of them went to college just to learn how to fix teeth, not how to grow a successful business. That's where I come in.

I've worked with over 5000 dentists all over the world in the past eight years to increase their profits – and with my vast experience, I've developed an enormous amount of exciting, proven methods that dentists, and even other businesses, can take advantage of …to make more money.

The title of this chapter is "The Hidden Goldmine in Your Business." By that I mean, most businesses already have the tools at their disposal to boost their profits in a substantial manner – they're just either unaware of those tools or simply not using them. My business is all about how to extract the most from that "Hidden Goldmine" – so that any business can prosper, even in tough economic times.

I'm going to share some of my top secret techniques that I use to help my dentistry clients boost their ROI a little later in this chapter, so hang on. They might just work for you, whatever business you're in!

FROM NURSE TO NICHE

When I went to college, I wanted a career that would enable me to be successful and help people. I chose nursing – but, as I was on the verge of finishing nursing school, I realized that would never be enough for me. I wanted to have my own business, not work for others.

I began reading many motivational books – especially those by Brain Tracy – and I decided that I wanted to be a motivational speaker, like Jack "Chicken Soup for the Soul" Canfield or Anthony Robbins. But cracking that market proved to be harder than I thought, and it taught me my first big business lesson; *you can be good at something, but it doesn't matter if you don't market or promote your business*.

That made me want to start studying marketing – and at an amazing moment. This was 2001 and internet marketing was still in its infancy. The potential, which is just being realized now, seemed tremendous. I began to learn about direct response marketing, and began selling coaching products online for one of my passions, volleyball.

Of course, you're not going to make a whole lot of money in the volleyball niche. But, again, I was just learning – and I noticed there were a lot of people online teaching others about how to make money in their particular professional niches. There were coaches for financial planners, real estate agents and other specific professions – it seemed to be a hot new trend.

I saw that this was a great field to get into – and after doing some more market research, I decided to jump full force into the dentistry niche. Why dentistry? Because, from my research, I knew that there were already a lot of dental practice consultants – so I knew there was a market for another one.

And this is where I'd like to share another valuable business lesson I've learned; when there's a lot of competition in a niche, that means there are a lot of people out there ready to buy. Many people shy away from a crowded field, thinking there's no room for a new person. Instead they put a lot of time and effort into a "breakthrough" business idea. The problem is, the odds are someone else already tried that breakthrough and found out there was no money in it – which is why no one else is doing it.

I always recommend finding a niche where the most buyers are, and then determining whether there's a way you can outmarket the existing sellers. If that way exists, you should get in and try it too. Targeting a proven money-making niche is a lot less risky (and a lot less exhausting) than creating a business from scratch.

Another thing that's important to realize is that you don't have to be an expert in a business in order to teach people how to 'grow' money in that business. Believe me, I have no idea how to fill a tooth or perform a root canal, but I do know how to help my dentist clients get more patients and make more money – and frankly, that's all they want and need me to do.

I've found that there are four aspects to a niche that make it attractive to market to:

1. The size of the niche – are there enough potential customers out there?
2. Who's currently selling to them? You have to see evidence that there is money to be made in the niche.
3. Will they want what you have to offer? There has to be a compelling reason people in this niche would buy your products or services.
4. Accessibility – is there an easy way to reach the niche base? Trade magazines and organizations are great methods to market to them.

Dentistry filled the bill in all these areas. I began Dentist Profits by spending 1800 dollars on a quarter-page ad in a dentistry trade magazine (today I would have done most of the initial marketing online). That ad immediately generated 42 leads and 7 sales. Those 7 sales at a thousand apiece meant I had made a good investment and that I had the beginnings of a great business – and eight years later, it's still paying off, for both myself and my clients!

THE MOST IMPORTANT MARKETING STEPS FOR A DENTAL PRACTICE

A huge chunk of the "hidden goldmine" in most dental practices comes from the fact that most dentists simply don't do any marketing to their patients, beyond a reminder postcard every six months to come in for a cleaning. 65% of all dental patients leave a practice because of apathy – they feel the doctors don't really care if they stay or go. That's a shocking and totally unnecessary drain on a practice.

It makes sense, then, that the easiest thing for a dentist to do is to make sure their patients know they *do* care. So the first thing I have a new client dentist do is send out a 3-step reactivation letter and postcard sequence to patients who haven't been in for awhile – with a very special offer attached. That offer could be a free whitening with their next appointment, a $100 credit towards cosmetic dentistry, or something similar. The point is to make a patient feel valuable through extending the offer. It's far easier, as most of you know, to sell to an existing customer rather than convert a new one, and it's the best and easiest way to immediately "jumpstart" a business increase.

The next step I recommend is implementing some kind of referral system

– by creating a "Care To Share" program. Dentists should ask existing patients to refer three friends to the practice – and give them referral cards with a Call to Action and a free offer attached (the patient ideally should get some kind of discount or deal for doing this). The most important part of this is that *the free offer should have a deadline for redemption within 30 days or less* – this motivates a new prospect to make the appointment rather than put it off.

A vital aspect of this referral program is that the dentist should designate someone else in the office to be solely responsible for it – someone who will report the number of referrals on a regular basis to the doctor and the rest of the practice team. This helps keep the momentum going and ensures that the necessary follow-up happens.

Another important way we help dentists increase profits – and another way our service is much different from other dental consultants - is that we help our clients niche market themselves. Just as I had to learn how to niche market myself to find a successful business, dentists also have to target the right patient base to grow their practices beyond the normal profit levels of a dental office. When a dental practice aims their marketing with a laser focus, rather than just throwing stuff at the wall to see what sticks, it allows for an overall increase in the dollar amount of each patient. Finding the right niche patient often means the difference between a practice not being profitable at all and being incredibly profitable.

One other vital way for a dental practice to push profits up is to open up and improve the new patient process - so that the staff is doing most of the presentation rather than the doctor. Some training has to happen to pull this off, but, once a dentist has this in place, they are 95 light years ahead of most practices out there!

PATIENT EVENTS

Want to make $100,000 more for a dental practice in one day?

Well, once the above ongoing marketing tools are in place at a practice, a dentist can do just that – by focus on holding special "Patient Events," which spur an immediate increase in patients and sales in a dramatic way. Not only that, they also help to make patients feel like the dentist is grateful for their business – the opposite of the kind of apathy that drives most patients away.

A "Patient Appreciation Day" does all that and more.

Here's an example of this kind of event. Let's say your niche is cosmetic dentistry. Who are your ideal patients? Females 35- 65. Well, what do they like to do? They like probably enjoy being pampered at a "girls' night out." So throw a women's night at a wine bar. Have a make-up artist there, maybe someone who does paraffin wax treatments and offer a special discount or free service for everyone who comes. Send the invite to your female patients – the only catch is that they have to bring two friends with them. That gives you every opportunity to convert their friends into new patients, especially if you offer them a special deal as well.

If you have a family practice, you might find throwing a Patient Appreciation Day in a park – or even just in your parking lot, if it's outside – also helps generate a lot of new business. Many of my clients do just that, and have a small petting zoo, a bouncy house, snacks and other fun stuff available at the event. We've had hundreds of people show up at some of these events, and they end up associating having a good time with a dental practice (which is not often the case!). Obviously, you make special offers available at this event as well to convert guests who aren't already patients.

A final great Patient Event idea is to take your 50 best patients out to a restaurant at the end of the year – in late November or early December, ideally. Again, you're showing them your appreciation - and you also can ask for referrals and testimonials, which gives you more marketing 'ammo' going into the New Year.

These are just a few of our creative marketing strategies that pay off in a big way for our clients. One of them – Dr. Scott Schumann, who had a chapter earlier in this book, went from doing 400,000 dollars a year to making over 2 million a year in just 3 years, during one of the worst recessions this country has ever been through. That's actually a great chapter to revisit – because Dr. Schumann also talks about how he uses Richard "The ROI Guy" Seppala's call-tracking systems to target his marketing more effectively. We've seen many clients triple their monthly business, just from implementing a consistent referral system and by having the dental staff learn how to properly market and present the practice to patients.

Whatever business you're in, I hope you can take away from this chapter that activity generates activity… and that nothing happens until something moves. If you're not out there marketing your business, or not trying something new to improve your bottom line, it's not going to happen.

So don't be afraid to try something for the first time. Go out there and do it and fail fast. Because the quicker you fail, the faster you succeed. 90% of the things you're going to learn come from the journey, from being willing to make mistakes, but keeping your eyes fastened firmly forward towards your goals.

Good luck to you all and I hope you've gotten some great tips from this chapter.

ABOUT ED

Known as an 'Outside-The-Box' money maker, Ed O'Keefe revolutionized how dentistry is marketed worldwide, building one of the largest coaching clubs. Ed is the real definition of an entrepreneur, owning multiple Internet businesses selling products that range from diet to fitness, how to make money online, & many more!

His best achievement is his 4 beautiful children & wonderful marriage to his wife. To get more information about Ed, you can find him at www.edokeefe.com

CHAPTER 18
INTERNET MARKETING BRINGS BUSINESS

by Tom Foster

There has been a major shift in the past several years regarding how consumers search for products and services. More and more people are gravitating to the Internet to find answers to their problems or more information regarding products and services. Will these consumers be able to find your business online?

The Internet is a powerful force that cannot be ignored. If you want to succeed in the current economic climate, then you need to allocate your time and money to your Internet marketing campaign.

In order to get the most out of Web marketing, you need to be able to accomplish the following:

1. Be found on pages 1 to 3 of all search engines *for every possible key phrasing* associated with your business.
2. You need to be able to convert search queries into visitors by getting people to click on your website link in the Google search listing, which will take them to one of your Web pages.
3. Once the online searcher has reached your website, you need to answer his or her question through your content and video.

IMPORTANCE OF SEARCH ENGINE OPTIMIZATION

Before you embark on your journey to develop a strong Internet marketing campaign that brings results, you need to understand search engine optimization (SEO). SEO can be defined as the process of improving your website's ability to be found organically by Google and other search engines. (When you hear the word "organic" in relation to search engines, it means that the website shows up naturally in search results due to content, links and other factors).

Your website needs to rank high in search engine results, because that is how your customers are going to find you. Below are some key facts that show the relevance of SEO:

- You can increase visitor traffic by 600 percent or higher if your website is listed at the top of organic search results.
- For the most part, organic rankings have higher quality traffic than pay-per-click listings.
- Potential customers will search for you by name and type of business.
- You can significantly boost your conversion rate by using targeted content and proper optimization.
- SEO can raise your online visibility in social media, blogs, press releases and more.

COMPONENTS OF A SUCCESSFUL INTERNET MARKETING CAMPAIGN

Now that you understand the relevance of search engine optimization, it is time to discuss what makes an Internet marketing campaign successful.

A. Good Content

Content is the best way to be discovered organically by search engines. Your website content incorporates your home page, articles, blog and any other Web pages on your site. The more content that you have on your website, the better your odds of attracting search engine traffic.

The content on your website will need to incorporate keywords and phrases that are related to your business or industry. Your key phrases should be in your page titles, content and in the descriptions of your pages. However, while there is no question that you need to write your content in such a way that it catches the attention of search engines (by including keywords), it also needs to make sense to your readers. So, in essence, you have to meet two goals with your content – to please the search engines and to satisfy your potential customers.

When creating your content, you need to think about what type of information will be important and of interest to your prospects. Content that answers questions and provides insight into solutions for your prospects' problems will draw people in. Be aware, though, that adding content to your website is not a one-time event. You need to continuously add fresh and unique content, if you want to continue ranking well among the search engines, and ultimately get in front of more prospects.

B. Link Building

Link building is a crucial element to SEO. You need to have inbound links throughout your website that point to interior pages, such as articles you have written, but you also need to have other, reputable sites, linking to yours. Links help improve your search engine ranking.

When it comes to links within your website, you can link your keywords to some of your other Web pages. For example, if you are an attorney, you might link the keywords, "Dallas accident attorney," to a page that discusses this practice area within your website.

The links pointing to your website are a major factor in search engine optimization, but you need to have the concept of "quality over quantity." The websites linking to your site should be related to your industry or location. You can increase the chances of getting these links by posting interesting content, including statistics, stories or even polls.

C. Web Video

Online video is the next big thing when it comes to marketing on the Internet. As YouTube and other sites continue to grow, so does the urgency to produce Web video. It has been estimated that 62 percent of Americans are watching videos on the Internet. That means that many of your potential customers are online looking for videos relating to your business.

Web video is a great conversion tool. People like to see and hear from you before contacting your office or walking into your store. Online video gives viewers the sense that they know you and can trust what you have to say. If you do not have online video on your website, then you are missing a great opportunity to get more business.

D. Call to Action

Once someone is on your website and has read or heard what you have to say, you need to give them a reason to contact you. Your website must have a *'call to action'*. While you can give them a *'call to action'* through a powerful headline or content, you can also create something that they can't live without. Free reports, books, CDs and other educational materials are great ways to get someone to contact you and say, "yes, I would like to get the conversation started, please send me your free book (or whatever you offer)." This type of conversion tool has been known to increase client bases by at least 60 percent.

E. Social Media

Social media offers more than just a way to stay connected with family and friends, it provides an outlet to get the word out there about your services or products. Social networking is huge and many retailers and small business owners have already jumped into this form of inexpensive marketing.

Social media websites, such as Twitter, Facebook and LinkedIn, will help you increase your online exposure. Imagine if someone searched your name after being recommended to your company by a friend and found your website, Facebook page, blog and LinkedIn profile! It would be pretty impressive.

By implementing these effective strategies to boost your visibility online, you will be able to maximize your marketing dollars, grow your business and watch your sales go up.

HOW FOSTER WEB MARKETING CAN HELP YOU

Foster Web Marketing is a full-scale Internet marketing boutique. We currently have over 200 clients and counting. Our dedicated team consists of some of the most talented designers, project managers, content writers, sales and customer service associates, and Web marketing professionals. We work closely with clients on a monthly basis to increase their online exposure and generate leads.

We have recently opened a video studio in Fairfax, Virginia, which is fully equipped with a green room and the latest editing and recording equipment to produce Web-friendly video solutions.

As the founder and president of Foster Web Marketing, I have created DSS (Dynamic Self-Service), a powerful and highly effective online application that allows our Web clients to update every aspect of their website themselves.

ABOUT TOM

Tom Foster is a highly reputable, nationally recognized Internet marketing specialist and published author who teaches successful Internet marketing strategies to organizations and businesses nationwide. He is the author of *Twitter for Attorneys*, *The 5 Biggest Mistakes 99% of Lawyers Make With Their Websites* and *How Smart Lawyers are Using Video on the Web to Get More Cases Without Breaking the Bank*, as well as the co-author of the best selling book, *Shift Happens: America's Premier Experts Reveal Their Biggest Secrets to Help You Thrive in the New Economy*. Tom has been featured in various publications, including *The Wall Street Journal* and *Newsweek* magazine.

Tom is the founder and president of Foster Web Marketing, which specializes in website design, search engine optimization, content management, Internet marketing strategies and more. Foster Web Marketing has designed and currently hosts websites for over 200 clients.

Since the company began in 1998, Foster Web Marketing's mission has always been to provide support and technical solutions for its clients, helping them get the most from new Web design technology that can improve long-term business performance of their organizations. By staying one step ahead of the technology curve and anticipating the business needs of its clients on a variety of levels, Foster Web Marketing has gained a solid reputation as a "secret weapon" for business owners.

CHAPTER 19
GETTING YOUR GOOGLE ON

by Brian Horn, Owner, Horndog Search Marketing

I want to thank Richard (ROI GUY) for allowing me to participate in this great book – because ROI is a subject near and dear to my heart.

For some reason, some people often forget how important ROI is to a business. They continue to put money into marketing maneuvers that simply don't work, just because they know they need to do *something* to get their name around. Unfortunately, they either don't have the time or don't do the research, to figure out what is the right marketing solution for their particular niche or business. What I provide to my clients is both the research and strategy essential to helping them succeed online – and I'm going to share some of my SEO secrets with you in this chapter.

I don't like to brag, but I believe I was born with an innate sense of ROI. You know how the X-Men in comic books and movies were all born with special super powers? It's kind of like that with me – only I can't read minds or fly or turn things to ice. No, I have the power of Entrepreneurship – which is kind of cool, but not exactly exciting enough for an action movie, because it's not all that helpful when battling super villains. But it was very helpful to *me*.

GROWING UP & GROWING BUSINESSES

I made my first move when I was in the fifth grade by starting a lawn mowing business in my hometown of Alvin, Texas, south of Houston (and the home of baseball great, Nolan Ryan). Yeah, a lot of kids make money mowing lawns – but not a lot of them take that money and invest it into a Champion Pedigree Dalmatian puppy. I raised and showed that beautiful award-winning pooch in a lot of shows - then I bred her several times and ended up earning over $20,000 raising and selling her puppies. That's a pretty good ROI considering I was only out the price of the pup, her dog food, some vet bills and a chewy toy or two.

In the ninth grade, I thought it was time to move from four-legged animals to the two-legged kind (I relate to them better). I took a portion of my Dalmatian dollars and invested it in a set of DJ equipment, then began a whole new business at the age of 14. I do have to say I couldn't have done it without my silent business partner – my mom, who would drive me and my stuff to every 'gig' in her blue and white Chevy Suburban.

As a matter of fact, that's when I learned one of the most important business lessons of my life – get the money upfront! When I got stiffed after a DJ 'gig', I made sure to get paid before I began spinning any tunes – and I have to say it's kind of fun shaking down forty year-old high school principals when you're only 14.

The DJ business was also very successful, and I expanded from just doing school dances and proms to weddings and corporate events. I was making over a $1000 a week just working Friday and Saturday nights – again a great ROI for only two nights of work (plus my Mom paid for the gas!).

Once I was in college, however, working weekend nights suddenly wasn't quite as much fun as it was when I was 14. I ended up selling the DJ business to a bigger Houston outfit - a final great pay-off from my initial investment in the necessary DJ equipment.

FINDING SEARCH MARKETING

Now, after that track record, you'd think that, after finishing college, I'd be off starting my own real grown-up business, right? Well, yes, it *would* have been right, but I chose to turn my back on what I did best and began working in the corporate sector. And even though it didn't satisfy my own personal ambitions, it did lead me to discover my current and very successful business niche in internet marketing.

I had worked my way up to Director of IT at the company I worked for - and realized it had a big problem. It was overwhelmingly paper-based in an increasingly online world (this was back in 2000, when the shift was in full swing). I took it upon myself to help the company make this urgent transition.

Soon I was reading every "…For Dummies" book available that had to do with web programming and the internet – and educating myself in a whole new arena of marketing I was barely aware existed...*Search Engine Optimization* (SEO). I discovered that by designing your site with certain structure and elements, you could raise your site's ranking in the search engines. And I instantly saw that this was an amazing field to get into – the field that would be the main marketing tool to my generation as well as a vital one to every age in the years to come.

After another stint at a digital marketing firm in Houston, I became a nationally-recognized expert in Search Engine Optimization – and began my own company, HornDog Search Marketing (growing up with the last name "Horn" you get stuck with that 'moniker' as a kid really fast…plus it makes a pretty memorable company name too). And I couldn't be more psyched about finally having my own business again. And what's really cool about it is that I don't even need my mom to drive me around to meet clients anymore.

Seriously, it's a huge understatement to say that a lot has happened in internet marketing in the past few years – it's an increasingly complex and challenging field that's constantly evolving. But it's also one that's filled with opportunity and nonstop excitement. The right step can make you millions – the wrong step can just leave you *lost* among the millions – the millions of other online marketers trying to make a name for themselves - just as you are.

That's why I work closely with my clients to make sure they're not spending a bundle on results that really aren't going to justify the expense. The ROI involved in your internet marketing has to make sense – just as it does in any bricks-and-mortar operation. You can't expect instant miracles just because you have a website you're 'throwing a bank vault full of money at'. You can, however, expect results that pay off - if you create an online strategy that makes sense in terms of your business plan, expenditures and execution.

DOLLARS TO DONUTS

One thing I do want to emphasize is that size *does* matter – especially when it comes to SEO. I worked hard with the After Bankruptcy Foundation on a massive project – to make sure their website came up on the first page of results from a Google search on the keyword, "Bankruptcy." How difficult was this job? Do a search on "Bankruptcy" yourself – and you'll come up with almost *53 million results*.

Now, you can imagine how many giant banks and financial firms want to own that valuable keyword – but there I was in my Cargo shorts and t-shirt, sitting in my home office, making it happen. It took a long time and a lot of my client's money – but, to achieve that incredible goal, that was what was needed.

Now let's flip that picture to a much smaller client with a much smaller budget – and, let's face it, can you get much smaller than a donut shop in Maine? I work with a restaurant marketer who was advising one, and they wanted their moment 'in the online sun' just as badly as the After Bankruptcy Foundation.

Fortunately, making a Maine donut shop an internet star isn't all that hard. By optimizing their online efforts so that the search term "Best Donut Shop in Maine" made them show up at the top of Google results. Then, a TV producer who was actually *looking* for the best donut shop in Maine, discovered our client and put their business on their show.

It's important to note that it was incredibly cost-effective to achieve that result – because there isn't a lot of competition for the keywords "Best Donut Shop in Maine." At the same time, there are tons of magazines, TV shows and even websites that love to feature the best "whatever" in "wherever" – so it's a great way to get attention to a smaller niche business.

MY SEO SECRETS

As you can see from the above examples, I work with clients of all sizes and needs. Primarily, I enjoy consulting with small businesses and entrepreneurs involved with Glazer-Kennedy marketing groups all across the country to make sure their internet marketing is targeted, effective, and they're getting an amazing ROI.

I'm not going to lie to you, however – the SEO process is an expensive one to pull off, in many cases. And it's not always a guarantee of success. It's something you have to commit to for at least a year to see the kind of results that make sense for an ongoing business. When it does succeed, it makes a huge impact for your business, however – and I have many success stories of making SEO work for my clients.

Basically, I begin by working out keywords with a client that will be effective in driving the desired traffic to their site. That involves a lot of research to see which keywords will bring in the most paying customers, but that also don't have an insane competition level from other businesses that are also using those keywords in their SEO efforts.

As a matter of fact, one of most effective ways to do that research is to actually see what's worked – and what *hasn't* worked – for rival online businesses similar to yours. An awesome tool for that is SpyFU, available at SpyFU.com. SpyFU enables you to actually see what keywords your competition is using, how effective they've been for them and how long they've been in use.

By looking at this information, you can see if a company has been consistently paying for a certain keyword for several years. If this same company has paid for, then stopped using other keywords…you know that those keywords won't pay off for you either.

As I noted earlier, many companies put money behind keywords without much thought or research – and you can learn a lot from their mistakes. You can also check out the ad copy they've been using and whether it's been effective. Especially if you're a start-up, SpyFU can jumpstart your research efforts by showing you the experience of other successful – and not-so-successful – businesses.

Once I've worked out which keywords we want to utilize with a client, we begin by testing those keywords in paid Google AdWords ads. These ads are displayed on top of and next to the organic results in Google, as you can see in the image at the top of page 139.

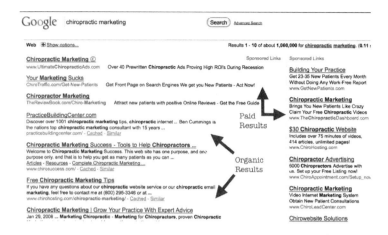

I create a squeeze page to send the paid ad traffic to. A squeeze page is just a one page website with an 'opt-in' form...usually the visitor can receive a free report or gift for giving their contact information. It's designed to give the visitor two options - leave their contact info…or leave the site. No navigation, limited content to read, etc., etc.

Squeeze Pages for the most part, across most niches, have the highest opt-in rate.

Here is a sample squeeze page:

Notice that there is very limited text…just a good headline, an offer for information in exchange for an email address, and some bullet points pointing out what is included in the free information. There is no navigation (except for Privacy Policy and Contact Us links…these are required by Google Adwords), nothing about the company or any other products or services.

We track the results from the squeeze page for about two weeks, which gives us the average cost per lead by keyword. This is the baseline we'll work from in going forward with this test.

We then do a side-by-side comparison of the landing page and the home page of a standard website by sending an equal amount of PPC traffic to each of them. This standard website will contain several navigation options, more general content, cover all the products and services available, etc.

Now, the landing page will win almost every time because it's more targeted towards a specific desire on the part of the web surfer. There's just one thing they can do…fill out that 'opt-in' form. Whereas the regular website has a multitude of options…click on the "About Us" page, scan the "Products" or "Services", read customer testimonials, check out hours of operation, etc. And the landing page is not selling them on your product or service…you are just selling them on your "free report" or whatever 'carrot' you're using.

You see, there's nothing wrong with visitors spending time on your website, but you primarily want their contact information, so you can add them to your marketing funnel and follow up if they don't buy from you today. That's what makes the squeeze page so powerful.

In this test, let's say the landing page got a 15% opt-in rate and the website got a 5% 'opt-in' rate.

At this point we ran the test side-by-side for 2 weeks. We'll say that we were paying an average of $5 per click, and we bought 1000 clicks over the course of those 2 weeks for both the squeeze page and the website.

Now let's look at the numbers:

Landing Page:
1000 clicks x $5 click = $5000 total spent
1000 clicks x 15% opt-in rate = 150 leads
$5000 total spend / 150 leads = $33.33 per lead

Website:
1000 clicks x $5 click = $5000 total spent
1000 clicks x 5% opt-in rate = 50 leads
$5000 total spend / 50 leads = $100.00 per lead

That tells us what our key numbers are. We know that if we have our website appearing in the organic listings, we can expect a similar opt-in rate. We also know how much a lead is worth, how many leads we can expect each week, and, by using all this information, we can determine how much we can spend on SEO and still get a positive ROI from our efforts.

Let's continue with this example.

If we get the site to rank in the top 3 positions in Google, we can expect, in most cases, about a 20% lift in clicks versus the top PPC spots. In the prior PPC example we were getting 1000 clicks every 2 weeks, so we can expect to have about 1200 from an organic listing.

We can expect the same 5% 'opt-in' rate, so we'll assume that the organic listing will bring in about 60 leads every 2 weeks. Since these are organic listings, you are not paying anything per click or per lead.

Back in the Landing Page example, we ended up paying $33.33 per lead. So if we are getting 60 leads per week, and *not* paying for them, they have a value of almost $2000.

Since that was for a 2 week period, multiply by 26 to get the value of a year ($2000 x 26 = $52,000).

Now we can take that number and know exactly how much our SEO budget should be, and if top organic rankings are worth pursuing.

GETTING YOUR GOOGLE ON

There are two primary ways of making sure your website ranks high on Google's results page – through properly structuring and optimizing your website and by building a strong link profile (getting links to your website placed on other websites).

"On Page Optimization" is what we call the first method, which consists of using keyword-rich content, structuring your site in a hierarchal method, using proper title and meta tags, and many other tools. You have to use the keywords in *legitimate content* (Google's pretty fast at catching a whole webpage of nothing but keywords repeated over and over), such as blogs, articles and your actual website copy.

The most popular way to work those keywords in, as well as establish your authority in your particular business niche, is by authoring and posting blogs and articles on relevant topics. For instance, if you're selling a vitamin supplement, you would obviously write about health issues that are conducive to working in keywords as often as possible.

Your best base of operations for this kind of blog and article posting is using the free content management system (CMS) available through Wordpress.com. You will probably want to either redesign one of their provided templates yourself or hire a web designer to do it - but the great thing is that after the initial page design is done, using the page is free, it's easy to post new content yourself, and you can link it to your own web address. This lowers your ongoing content management costs to almost nothing - and Wordpress is a very professional and popular CMS to work with.

You may be too busy to blog more than a couple of times a week – most entrepreneurs are. You can certainly hire a good freelance writer to 'ghostwrite' for you to help keep your content fresh and add to the keyword count.

You can also open your blog to outside contributors as well – making sure nothing gets posted without your approval, of course. By inviting others in your niche to blog, you begin to create your own business network - as well as getting free and informative content on your site. Another benefit is that when you let someone else provide content for your blog, they almost always will email their list of customers, family, friends, etc and let them know to go check out their post on your blog. This means free traffic for you! Always a good thing, right?

They most likely will link to it from their site also… this is a VERY good thing for SEO too. So let's explore why that link is so beneficial to your SEO efforts.

STRONG LINKS MAKE A STRONG CHAIN

As I mentioned earlier, there are two primary ways to make sure your website ranks high on a Google search. We've just touched on the first method of On Page Optimization – but the important thing to realize about that method is that it's only responsible for 10 to 20% of what makes your website rank in Google. The other way, Off Page Optimization, contributes *over 80%* of what causes your website to rank high.

Off Page Optimization, also known as Link Building, is obtaining links to your website on other influential and recognized websites. It's clearly your biggest weapon – and your biggest challenge – when it comes to improving your Google ranking. You can hire Link Building experts to help you in this effort – or you can take on the job yourself. You can also use Link Brokers to buy links for you on other sites – even though Google says this is a no-no, it's almost mandatory to build your online profile in a competitive niche.

There are a few easy ways to begin this process.:

1. Write and submit articles to article directory sites like EzineArticles. com, GoArticles.com and Buzzle.com.
2. Submit your content to social bookmarking services like Delicious, Digg, Reddit, Stumble Upon, etc.
3. Comment on blogs that allow you to put a link back to your site at the end of your comment.
4. Write testimonials for your vendors in exchange for a link back to your site.
5. Get listed in directories in your business' niche. The easy way to find these is to google your niche and the word "directory". So if you are a dentist, you would google "dentist directories."

These are some basic ways to start building your link profile. But, your main priority will be getting your links placed on quality sites that Google acknowledges are leading online resources for your particular niche.

This is a tremendously productive and powerful strategy. For example, if you're working in the nursing industry, Nurse.com is the site to go after. The best way to get a link back to your website from such a high-level site, is to be allowed to post content that contains a link back to your site.

How do you get the all-clear from these sites to post your own content? Here's my simple trick – and it has never failed to deliver for me yet. And believe it or not, it involves going offline to get the job done.

What I do is obtain the mailing address for these sites and I create a simple direct mail piece to send to them. I'll usually put in a simple clever gift or some other way of getting their attention – because putting in this kind of personal effort means a big pay-off later, as you only need a few of these sites to cooperate with you to make a big difference in your results from Google . I also provide some sample content in the mailing so they know I actually can deliver what I'm promising.

With the gift, I write a request asking that they allow me to contribute some content to their site. And I'm specific. I look over the site, see where they might need some additional content that they don't currently have, and offer to cover that particular area.

I don't ask for a link back at this time….just offer to give them free quality content. Once they accept my offer, I'll slip in the request for a link. My version of the "Columbo Technique."

Again, I've never been turned down on this request. The fact that I would actually take the trouble to *mail* something – yes, the Post Office still does deliver things to people – makes me stand out when most people are deleting marketing email after marketing email from their inbox. Some people spend thousands and thousands of dollars to make this happen – all you have to do is come up with some clever personalized direct mail piece for three or four websites.

(And, by the way, to return to my previous suggestion about soliciting contributions from other online marketers to bolster your own site's content? Offering to allow a link back to *their* site is a great inducement to get them to follow through with that content.)

DOING YOUR OWN FOLLOW-UP

Once you've begun to work on your site's SEO marketing, it's important to track your efforts and see what's working – and what's not. Remember when I advised you to research your competition 's websites? Now it's time to do that to yourself – and a great free tool to use for that purpose is Google Analytics (available at: http://www.google.com/analytics).

Track your own ROI and find out which organic search terms are bringing in traffic. See if those visitors are actually paying customers or just generated leads – also analyze what they actually do when they come to your site. Are they immediately leaving – or are they sticking around to check out other pages? Which pages are they visiting? Answering questions like these help you optimize your site to maximize your conversion rates and your ROI – and they're the kind of answers I provide to my clients, along with solutions to their particular online challenges.

Search Marketing is a huge subject, much too huge for one chapter. There are plenty of paid courses, webinars and training DVDs available that can help you if you want to pursue doing it yourself. Outsourcing your SEO efforts will probably guarantee more profitable results, but is also obviously a lot more expensive. Again, it's a matter of whether outsourcing will end up paying for itself in increased online revenue. That's something I always discuss upfront with any potential client.

The internet will continue to evolve and change – and so will Search Marketing. Stay on top of the latest trends, as well as Google's evolving methods, and you'll stay on top of the online game. And please feel free to contact me at: brian@horndogsearch.com if I can be of any assistance to you. Even if you just need a good DJ. Just remember – cash up front!

ABOUT BRIAN

Brian Horn is recognized by many as the "Glazer-Kennedy Secret Weapon" because of his role in helping not only Dan Kennedy and Bill Glazer with search engine optimization and social media, but also many of their Platinum coaching clients and some of the top Information Marketers in the world. These marketers include such leaders as Ali Brown, Ed O'Keefe, Chris Cardell, Stephen Snyder, Rory Fatt, Vickie Milazzo, Scott Tucker, Dean Cipriano, Steve & Bill Harrison, Dennis Tubbergen, Ron Caruthers, Michael Gravette, Jimmy Vee & Travis Miller. Brian has also consulted with US Congressional Candidates and a current Lieutenant Governor. Brian has consulted with these marketing titans in secrecy for nearly 5 years...his name being passed along in the strictest of confidence only to a select few. Brian's system famously got a client on page 1 of Google for the 7th most searched term of the year in only 8 months. Additionally, Brian's system got one client to page 1 of all the search engines for every competitive term in their niche...and sales exploded from $0 to over $4 million in just 9 months.

In his heart, Brian is an entrepreneur's kinda guy. You see, Brian understands entrepreneurs, because he has been one himself since the 5th Grade, when he started a lawn mowing business one summer in his hometown of Alvin, TX. Brian invested the money he earned in a Champion Pedigree Dalmatian puppy. He raised, and showed the dog, then eventually had her bred several times and earned over $20,000 raising and selling puppies. He saved a portion of the money, and invested part in equipment for a DJ company he started in the 9th grade. Brian quickly went from playing school dances and parties to weddings and corporate events. By the time he was in college, Brian was earning over $1,000 a week working just Friday's and Saturday's. Brian continued as a DJ through college, before selling the business to a larger Houston-based company.

CHAPTER 20
RAMP UP YOUR "ROO!"

by Lindsay Dicks

No, the title of this chapter isn't a misprint. And I know this is Richard Seppala's book and he's the ROI Guy, not the ROO Guy. But ROO is what I want to talk about.

Why? Well, "ROO" means "Return on *Objective*." And in the world of social media, it's a much more practical way to look at and accurately measure the impact of what you're doing.

ROI implies very black-and-white dollars-and-cents results. In other words, "We put this much money into this marketing campaign – so how much money did we make from that investment?"

Well, social media isn't that simple. First of all, many of the things you do on social media are hard to directly measure in terms of monetization. Usually, you're not asking directly for the sale, because it's not the most effective use of social media – but, if you're doing it correctly, <u>you *are* driving the kind of quality traffic to your website and your business, that will result in generating new leads and increased revenues.</u>

Second of all, many of the things you do on social media *don't cost anything*. If you're doing your own Facebook and Twitter posts, it's not like making a radio buy or a newspaper placement – <u>it's *free*</u>, ...aside from the costs of running and maintaining an effective social media-friendly website (as we're happy to do for you at CelebritySites™).

While social media can definitely make you money, it's difficult to put an exact dollar value on what it costs or what it makes. That's why, instead of trying to measure your ROI, you should measure your ROO. (Or if you're really thorough, go ahead and measure both – but we'll get to that later.)

YOUR SOCIAL MEDIA OBJECTIVES

Since we're dealing with objectives instead of dollars, obviously, the first step to measure your ROO is to define what your objectives are when it comes to using social media. Here are a few common and powerful outcomes/objectives:

147

- **Boost Your Search Engine Results Rankings**

To show up in the first few results from a Google search, you need to be all over social media to make it happen. Creating online conversations and having your name and website links pop up wherever possible is key to making you "pop."

- **Provide Third Party Verification**

When people Google your name and find other people talking about you and endorsing you, as well as your articles and videos on other reputable sites, you become more credible. Social media makes that happen.

- **Make You The "Star" Of Your Field**

The more buzz you create, the more content you post, the more you are at the center of online conversations, the more you appear to be the authority in your particular expertise.

- **Lead Generation**

Because you make yourself the star of your industry, because you boost your credibility as well as your search engine ranking, more people interested in what you have to offer will visit your website, and respond to your Call to Action (an offer designed to get them to leave their contact information), giving you quality leads that are likely to buy! These people *already know who you are* from your social media marketing – you've presold the kind of clients you want to attract.

- **Increased Sales**

Social media is still ALL about making you more successful – in a more concrete and lasting way than just emailing a single sales letter to people who may not know you at all. When your name sparks instant recognition to an internet user, you're way ahead of the game – and much more likely to be able to close a sale with a customer who might be skeptical of a competitor they only know from a "brochure" website or 'sales pitch'. It's a way to create a relationship before there's even any selling involved – or even you being directly involved!

TRACKING YOUR ROO

A lot of the objectives I listed above can be analyzed through various measurements that will give you a good idea of how effective your social media is – we do it all the time at CelebritySites™. The good thing about any online activity is that it's easy to track through Google Analytics and other internet tools – and here are some important aspects of your website traffic to look at, before and after you implement social media marketing:

- **Repeat Visitors**

Are visitors beginning to come back repeatedly to your site to view new content and check out any updates? Growing return traffic means you're growing a strong base.

- **Comments on Your Blogs**

Are you generating any conversation with your content? If you are, you should be entering into the conversation by replying to the comments. If you're not, you might want to reevaluate your content to see if it's interesting enough to the average visitor.

- **Length of Time Your Visitors Stay on Your Website**

The longer people stay during a visit to your website, the bigger the impact on your Google search ranking. Constant new and updated content, and especially video, can really help grow this number.

- **Number of Newsletter Subscriptions**

Are you generating more subscribers as a result of your social media marketing? You should be if you're doing it right – because more people will be interested in what you have to say and what you have to offer

- **Number of Downloads**

If you offer any free downloads (special reports, eBooks, etc.), monitor if the number is going up. Again, it should be increasing as your online reputation builds and your influence grows.

- **Referring Sites**

The list of sites that your own website traffic is coming from should begin to grow, which in turn should be increasing your overall traffic numbers. Not only that, you should also be able to tell which social media is doing you the most good, i.e. generating the most traffic to you, so you might want to focus on those areas.

REMEMBER…YOU CAN MEASURE ROI TOO!

Now that I've walked you through ROO, I do have to admit – there are ways to measure your ROI too! These are methods to determine which specific campaigns and 'landing' pages generated the most leads – and the most sales. They're generally used more for targeted sales offers than for general social media content – but they are readily-available tools that can help you measure the dollars and cents aspects of your internet marketing.

- **Toll-Free Hotline Numbers**

Richard "The ROI Guy" Seppala has written about how to use these toll-free numbers elsewhere in this book. To sum it up, he will provide you with

149

different numbers to put on different online campaigns. You can track how well each of these campaigns is doing instantly. Richard also provides a way to capture the contact information of each generated lead that calls, as a result of your campaign or ad.

- **Individual URLS**

You can assign different URL or domain names as links for different campaigns, even though they may take the prospect back to the exact same page. This works similar to the toll-free hotline numbers, in that you can see which campaign drives the most traffic.

- **Using CTA's**

Implementing a strong CTA, or "Call To Action," where you offer some sort of time-limited free information, can motivate a visitor to "opt-in" and leave their contact information on your site. This allows you to build a database to market to, and also reflects whether your online marketing is effective or not.

ROO 101: A TUTORIAL OF SORTS

Let's walk through a sample scenario to see just how social media can generate an awesome ROO.

And to make it fun – for me, at least! – let's set it in the world of fashion design.

Say up-and-coming *fashionista* Jenny Roo is trying to establish herself as the Shoe Guru – the one source for the all season's hottest, most wanted, completely 'die-to-have-them' shoes. She wants customers to be banging down her door (or maybe filling up her inbox) with requests for the hard-to-find and limited edition styles only she can track down. Of course, as a true *fashionista*, Jenny can't keep from buying a few of those one-of-a-kind finds for herself. So she has some work to do.

She checks on GoDaddy.com and discovers the ShoeGuru.com domain is available. Then she builds a website around it. And she has the good sense (and of course, good taste) to hire us at CelebritySites.com to put together the site for her.

Her objectives?

- To generate new leads
- To establish herself as the "Shoe Guru" that the rest of the *'fashionista* community' turns to for the hottest new shoes.
- To get testimonials from third parties to give her credibility

We built Jenny's website and make it social media-friendly, by including:

- Researched keywords that are popular in Google searches and targeted meta-data to the 'designer shoe' niche
- A Bio

- A FAQ page
- An introductory video from Jenny welcoming people to her site
- Updated blogs and articles on the latest trends in shoes, up and coming designers, shoe news and other shoe-related content
- A "Call to Action" offering a free downloadable report, "Fall 2010 Shoe Report" complete with a coupon for $50 off any pair of shoes ordered through her site – in return for a visitor's email address (Jenny will also send them her free Shoe Trends News ezine, professionally produced by us, every month)
- An auto-responder sequence set up to go out to the email addresses that the opt-in free report gathers
- Links to Jenny's Twitter, Facebook, Flickr and YouTube accounts, as well as the option to "opt-in" to Jenny's RSS feed
- Social bookmarking icons - so users can flag Jenny's content on Digg, Delicious, StumbleUpon, Reddit and more, and boost her overall on-line presence.

We also create a press release announcing Jenny's new Shoe Guru website and Shoe Search System. We syndicate it, along with Jenny's blogs and articles, to a ton of other websites and publications.

It turns out local style star Laura, surfing the web on her iPhone, gets Jenny's Tweet, "Must-Have Shoes for Fall + $50 off designer shoes" at: www.ShoeGuru.com," and is 'psyched' to have found a new shoe source. She, it turns out, has 'scored' amazing shoes from Jenny before. She retweets it to all her best *fashionista* friends, adding that Jenny is her most trusted style source for shoes. Jenny direct-messages her back asking if Laura will provide a testimonial. She webcams herself telling the story of how, before a party last Christmas, Jenny 'scored' her a pair of limited edition Louboutins. She posts it on Jenny's Facebook page.

A few days later, Eric, a style-conscious guy (yes, there are some out there), is looking for a unique pair of shoes for a party – maybe an online specialist could help track down something great? He Googles "mens designer shoe finder" and ShoeGuru.com comes up at the top of the results. He heads over to the site and sees Laura's enthusiastic video testimonial, which we have placed on Jenny's home page. He immediately downloads the report and coupon. When he spots a pair of very limited edition suede Gucci slip-ons, he puts in a request for Jenny to track them down.

Voila - the social media delivered an incredible ROO and Jenny is at the beginning of becoming an online sensation!.

Social media can do the same for you, giving you both the ROO and the ROI you're after. So, if you're ready to ramp up your ROO, all of us here at CelebritySites™ are ready to help! As Jenny will tell you, *'if the shoe fits – you should wear it'*, or as Cinderella says- ***"one shoe can change your life!"***

ABOUT LINDSAY

Lindsay Dicks helps her clients tell their stories in the online world using social media powered websites and multi-channel marketing tools. Being brought up around a family of marketers, but a product of Generation Y, Lindsay naturally gravitated to the new world of online marketing. Lindsay began freelance writing in 2000 and soon after launched her own PR firm that thrived by offering an in-your-face "Guaranteed PR" that was one of the first of its type in the nation.

Lindsay's new media career is centered on her philosophy that "people buy people." Her goal is to help her clients build a relationship with their prospects and customers. Once that relationship is built and they learn to trust them as the expert in their field then they will do business with them. Using Social Media and Search Engine Optimization, Lindsay takes that concept and builds upon it by working with her clients to create online "buzz" about them to convey their business and personal story. Lindsay's clientele span the entire business map and range from doctors and small business owners to Inc 500 CEOs.

Lindsay is a graduate of the University of Florida with a Bachelors Degree in Marketing. She is the CEO of CelebritySites™, an online marketing company specializing in social media and online personal branding. "The biggest mistake people make online is believing that their website is just an extension of their business cards and brochures. That approach is not only old fashion; today it's a waste of time and money. Your website has to be dynamic, grab attention, tell a compelling story and ultimately convert visitors into prospects and finally into customers. If not, that traffic that you've worked so hard to get to your website will move on within 10 seconds, never to be seen again. We help our clients avoid that pitfall to grow their business and their revenue streams."

Lindsay is co-author of the best-selling books, "Big Ideas for Your Business" and "Shift Happens." She was also selected as one of America's PremierExperts™ and has been quoted in Newsweek, the Wall Street Journal and USA Today, as well as featured on NBC, ABC, FOX and CBS television affiliates speaking on social media, search engine optimization and making more money online.

CHAPTER 21
BECOME AN ONLINE AUTHENTIC AUTHORITY

by Ian Garlic

Tiger Woods. I can hear all of you sighing as you mutter, "Do we have to talk about Tiger Woods *again*?"

Well, we don't *have* to. But I'd like to.

Because there's an important point about what happened to the world's greatest golfer, in terms of what I advise my clients. In Tiger's case, when his scandals became public, the media circus was incredibly huge and the internet talk was all-pervasive. And it wasn't just because he was having sex with several women other than his wife (although, yeah, that *contributed*).

No, it was because his image was completely fabricated in the first place.

Tiger Woods was perceived as a 'squeaky clean' family man who was so decent that he was almost boring. That's because that's how his handlers coached him to act in public early on in his career. He had nice, polite press conferences and almost never engaged in any controversial behavior in front of the cameras.

The *shock* of much of that image being a lie is really what the story was all about. A lot of other sports superstars engage in behavior that's just as bad, if not worse – and while their various wild nights will merit a story or two, it's nothing like what Tiger Woods endured.

The lesson, to me, is that even someone who crafts an image as carefully as Tiger is due to fail spectacularly at some point – because it's not an *authentic* image. He ended up with the worst possible online (and offline) "conversation" about himself – and it ended up costing him millions upon millions of dollars in endorsements and business, not to mention his having to temporarily withdraw from professional golf until the 'media storm' passed.

It's great to be successful. But it's horrible to fall so far so fast. That is why I preach to my clients the need to be an "Authentic Authority." I give those clients, most of whom are attorneys, doctors and other upscale professionals, the tools to leverage their "internet capital" - in order to establish themselves at the center of just the opposite kind of social media conversation – one that helps

153

them establish themselves as reliable experts, the 'real deal' who can provide information and advice in ways that inform and help *their* clientele. It helps them cement a favorable image that's genuine in the online community – it helps build their customer base - and it also comes back to boost their standing in Google search results.

Let's look at how that can happen for you.

KEEPING IT REAL ONLINE

Earlier, I mentioned "internet capital" – that's what you have to "spend" to create an impressive online presence. There are 4 pieces of internet capital that you generally have to work with:

1. Online links back to your website and social media pages
2. Your URL – which is your "real estate"
3. Your main marketing message or concept
4. Your online reputation – what people know about what you do, how you do it and what you're capable of doing

When I start with a new client, I get to know his or her business until I understand what it's all about. And that's what we build on – a *genuine* representation and projection of who they are and what they have to offer. We call it "authentic web marketing" – because we don't believe in making up stories about them and their business. And we carry that image throughout all aspects of their online capital – their website, their blogs and other web content, and their social media. It's always more powerful when everything works together – but what makes it really strong is the *authenticity* behind it.

For those of you who equate marketing with creative lying, it's really not the way to go when you're creating an image for yourself and/or your business. Once you start putting out information that doesn't 'jive' with reality, just because you think that's the image people are going to buy, you end up attracting the kind of clients you don't really like, you dilute your brand, you risk a Tiger Woods-like backlash should conflicting information surface, and ultimately it doesn't work.

Especially with social media being so popular today – where anyone can say anything about you. These are powerful venues that we train our clients to use in order to maximize their online impact. Coming from a place of truth means their clients will validate them through Facebook and Twitter. Those kinds of impromptu "testimonials" are the strongest positive online marketing you can generate.

As a search engine specialist, I've found that using social media correctly can help a professional dominate Google search rankings in their area, as well as become an "Authentic Authority."

GROWING UP WITH SOCIAL MEDIA

My experience with computers goes back to when I was 7 years old and my parents put me into a college-level computer programming class. And whatever basic form of social media existed at the time, I participated in. I grew up with the internet, going on bulletin boards back in 1990. And one of the most exciting days of my life was when I finally got a 96 kbps dial-up modem. I was on LinkedIn from day one in 2003, using it to connect and get connected to people when I worked in commercial real estate in New York City, and, naturally, when Facebook and Twitter became powers to be reckoned with, I was all over them figuring out how they worked and how to make the biggest impact on them.

I also worked for Thomson Reuters to help create websites for lawyers. For years, I helped attorneys get to the top of search engine results. That's when I really learned how to best market a professional on the internet – and I realized that nobody was out there offering the kind of overall online expertise that was needed not only by lawyers, but also by dentists, doctors, entrepreneurs and others running their own businesses.

Social media was a critical part of this strategy - because it's important to achieve great search engine results. These days, SEO (Search Engine Optimization) only gets you so far – the trick is to get social media to finish the job as well as establish you as an Authentic Authority in your field.

You have to view online conversations through such vehicles as Facebook and Twitter as cocktail parties, where your name gets out there and stays out there. You augment and build on the conversation *you* start, adding links back to your website and your blog, and you do that by making it about who you're talking to, rather than just about you.

What business people do the most on the internet is probably the *least* important thing in terms of helping their business – talking about themselves, what they're doing, what they're after. To be honest, people don't care about what *you* want. They care about what *they* want. Helping to meet *their* needs elevates *your* stature in their eyes.

THE SIX RULES OF SOCIAL MEDIA

This is information my clients usually pay for, but I'm going to let you in on the six rules of using social media. I don't mind sharing it, because most of my clients are so busy, they don't really want to spend a lot of time doing it themselves. But I do coach them in the process, because it's important for them to understand what works to make them a more powerful online presence.

1. CONCENTRATE

This is the first big step - *listen*. Pay attention to what people are saying – and what they're searching for information on – on the internet. Use Google Analytics, Google searches, Twitter searches, etc. to see what the buzz is in your field and what needs are the biggest. This is how you find out what potential clients want.

2. CURATE – Organize and Oversee

Find things that relate to you and what you do, and that ties into the online buzz. There is so much great information out there that you don't even have to generate the content; you can just link to it on your website or on Facebook, etc. The important thing is that *you* are seen as the guru "discovering" this kind of information and putting it out there.

3. FACILITATE

Make it easy for people to access your information and get in touch with you – make it easy for your clients to share information about you. Make sure you have links back to your website when you post something, and links to your Twitter and Facebook accounts as well.

4. MEDIATE

Watch what people are saying about you or about something in your field and connect them. Become the center of the conversation. If people begin a chain of comments on a link you put on Facebook, put yourself in the middle of it. Cast yourself as the professional expert leading the conversations and you'll be seen in that light.

5. INITIATE

Once you've begun this process, you'll begin to sense certain undercurrents in the online conversation and you'll be able to "catch a wave," to use some surfing terminology. As you begin to see which clients or people of influence are important to cultivate relationships with in order to further your "Authentic Authority" image, initiate conversations with them to gather testimonials and create associations that will help both them and yourself.

6. CONSUMMATE

Always consummate the relationships you initiate. What does that mean? Well, you can look at online connections as being like "blind dates." And when you're ready to go "all the way," you take it offline. I'm not going back to any Tiger Woods jokes here – I just mean it's time to pick up the phone and actually talk to the person or drop a note in the actual, physical mail (the kind where you lick a stamp and put it on the postcard or envelope). Show they matter in your real life, not just your virtual one.

There are also other ways to consummate a relationship. For example, if I'm going to a seminar or meeting, I go online to see who else is going and I interact with them so we can meet up when we get there. That way I'm connected before I get there. If you have a lot of (hopefully, happy) clients going to a meeting, gather them together for your own offshoot get-together where, again, you're the center of the group. Get them excited about what you're doing and they'll begin adding links and content about you to their online social media and websites.

And don't forget to use video as much as possible. Have your clients interviewed as they're leaving your office for testimonials – you might think they'll be too shy to do it, but most love it. As a matter of fact, they'll start bugging you about when you're going to post their video! Interview your staff too – it helps the people who come in to your office or practice to know them better and regard them as family. That, in turn, further cements their bond to you.

Use video for yourself as well. I have a client who did a video just talking about what she did and her track record – then she posted it on Facebook. People who had known her for years didn't actually know what she did – and were suddenly impressed. She gets a steady stream of referrals because of the video and, in one week, she got four new clients because of it.

The more social media you do, the more you create your Authentic Authority. When your patients or clients come to see you, talk to them about LinkedIn and Facebook and how they help your business. Get as many people to participate that are glad to be in your circle as possible.

The results will amaze you. Not only will you end up dominating searches in your area for your profession, you will also build a solid, ongoing reputation as a leader in your field.

Before social media, networking was done strictly through phone calls and get-togethers, where the impression you made and the word-of-mouth you got was dependent on people's usually-bad memories. Now, all your hard networking work lasts online – and allows you to build a visible "back catalog" of information, achievements and testimonials that's accessible to all. The more you do, the more you end up with. And the fact that most of it costs almost nothing, means it can't help but bring you a tremendous ROI.

Keep it real. Keep it going. And you can be the star of your own social media conversation.

ABOUT IAN

Ian Garlic has been working with computers since he took his first programming class in 1980. He started connecting with people on BBS' (Bulletin Board Systems, the online precursor to all social media in the late '80s) - when CompuServe was the internet, and has been hooked ever since.

Ian graduated from Rollins College in Winter Park FL in 1997, moved to New York City in 2003, and recently relocated back to Orlando to be close to family and friends.

He has worked in marketing and online development online brokerages, law firms, hedge funds, commercial real estate and the hospitality industry before evolveALOUD. Ian has found that the most important thing is that people are all the same. They have a fear of the unknown and want to be a part of something. The Internet allows him to help with those basic needs and aid Authentic Businesses in growing. He feels that when people seek out information and friendship on the web, it gives business the perfect place to truly market and innovate, not just advertise and hope.

Now evolveALOUD combines SEO, Social Media and Online Video Strategies into a synergistic inbound campaign. Ian develops online presences and inbound marketing for small biz and professionals such as Lawyers, Dentists, Doctors and Photographers with his Authentic Web Marketing Company, evolveALOUD. He also consults with major corporations and teaches workshops on the subject. The power is now there for small businesses to market and compete on a global scale and evolveALOUD accelerates that power in the most innovative, effective ways.

His team's vision is lead by a quote from Peter F. Drucker: **"Business has only two functions - marketing and innovation ... Everything else is an expense..."**

To quote Ian: "I really wouldn't say I have free time, but I try to incorporate as much cooking, eating and golf into our business development as is possible."

CHAPTER 22
THE HIDDEN GOLDMINE IN YOUR BUSINESS

by Timothy Seward, CEO, ROI Revolution, Inc.

I f you put a dollar into a vending machine, and received three dollars back...how many more dollars would you put into it?

Your answer would probably be... every dollar you had.

That's an apt metaphor for what we work towards with all our clients – to make their online marketing a money machine where, the more dollars you put in, the more you get out. We've spent a lot of years at ROI Revolution amassing the experience, the expertise and the data-crunching technology to become one of the premier Search Engine Marketing firms in the world.

Pay-Per-Click (PPC), is an internet advertising model that gives large and small advertisers the opportunity to bid on keywords and show up on major search engine (Google, Yahoo, MSN/Bing) results. Advertisers specify the amount they are willing to pay per click (or a visit to their website) and only pay when a searcher clicks on their ad.

It's such an exacting art/science, that changing a few words in a text ad can cause dramatic increases in response – or dramatic decreases. We're not always sure why something works or doesn't work, but we always want to find out *what* works – so your online campaigns can succeed and scale the way you want them to.

We've focused our practice solely on SEM (Search Engine Marketing). We don't do SEO (Search Engine Optimization) or email marketing. We are totally data-driven, while also working with our clients to ensure their landing page optimization is as high as possible to help their sites convert better. We align our goals with our clients' goal – which is to make more money for them.

I probably don't have to tell you that Search Engine Marketing gets more competitive every single day. That means that the importance of managing your campaigns at the highest possible level absolutely also grows every single day.

THE ROOTS OF THE "ROI REVOLUTION"

My name is Timothy Seward and I'm the founder and CEO of ROI Revolution. I first really got into numbers and data when I ran a brick-and-mortar business, a wholesale automotive accessories distribution company. With the help of my business partner, who was an engineer, we built the company up to 55 employees and six million dollars in annual revenue.

Our business was twice as profitable as the national average for our kind of business – and I attribute a lot of that to automating our sales and marketing operation as fully as possible in the 1990's. With a 25 user computer network, we employed a sophisticated accounting system where we could know the revenue and even gross profit per customer or per sales person from the previous day each morning – something that sounds simple now, but wasn't so simple then.

Using data like that was what really intrigued me, and, when I got a buyout offer for the business in the late '90's, I sold my shares and decided to go back to school full time for a bachelor's degree in Computer Science.

When I graduated in December of 2001, I was preparing to move from Florida to Raleigh, North Carolina, to start up a tech firm in order to leverage what I had learned in my college courses. I chose Raleigh due to its proximity to several large colleges and universities. And it was that move which really gave me a preview of how powerful the Internet had become.

I decided to sell my Florida home myself "by owner" and use some online marketing in the mix – something not commonly done at that time in the real estate market. I ran some Google ads and some "pop-under" banner ads, all of which advertised our home for sale by owner.

During our open house weekend, we ended up having 132 families come through our home, with at least half the traffic generated by my online ads. The family who ended up buying our house saw my internet ad from his home in Long Island, NY, and actually flew down to Naples, FL, with his wife for the open house. He ended up putting in the highest offer for our home on Sunday night and went under contract Monday morning – when they flew back to Long Island! That would *not* have happened if I hadn't advertised online.

The process of selling our home by owner using heavy Internet advertising was such an unusual event that two local TV stations came to cover the sale – and it was a huge revelation for me, opening my eyes to the power of the Internet as a direct response medium that had really come of age.

WHAT THE ROI REVOLUTION IS ALL ABOUT

My objective, when I started ROI Revolution, was to enable online marketers to drive qualified traffic to their website – and harness the power of the Internet to really grow their business.

Google launched their PPC model AdWords™ in February of 2002 –

and I started running PPC ad campaigns just 2 months later, in April of that same year.

At first, my company did a little bit of PPC, some web design and we would track our clients' success with Webtrends software. Webtrends was one of the first website analytics tracking softwares and provided great in-depth analysis, which I found endlessly fascinating.

Over the years, we became experts in Google AdWords and Analytics, to the point where our work has been featured in at least four books on the subject. We currently have 28 employees, with 2 more coming on board soon, and a little over 80 clients in 5 different countries (the U.S., Canada, the UK, Australia and Spain).

A large part of our client satisfaction has come from my philosophy of no outsourcing – my in-house staff does all the work for our clients. Each of my employees is required to spend at least six hours per month educating themselves: studying industry blogs, reading applicable books or attending online trainings. Because we allow ourselves that time, and because we do all the work ourselves, we can often identify breakthroughs and trends when they're in the early stages—to help our clients scale their success faster than their competitors. Furthermore, we are obsessive about developing in-house tools and software to help leverage the time we spend working on our clients' PPC accounts—so they can get more results in each hour of our work.

Generally, we have two distinct levels of clients that we provide services for – experienced online marketers and beginners.

IMPROVING ONLINE MARKETERS' PROFITS

The experienced online marketers have generally been operating a website for 3 years or more. They've either been directly selling 'stuff' online, generating leads to their sales staff who follow up with a phone call or a personal visit, or generating leads through an 'opt-in' or autoresponder to get them in their sales loop.

This group of businesspeople is typically already spending five to ten thousand a month or more on Google AdWords. They're making money; they just do not have time to manage their campaigns anymore, while, at the same time, costs are getting higher because of the competition. They know that their campaigns could be made more cost efficient and then scaled – if so, they could profitably be doubling or tripling their revenues from online marketing.

They look to our company to take them to the next level, improve declining results, or just enhance the quality of their life so they don't have to feel like they need to work 24/7 on their online campaigns.

The first thing we typically do with this level of client is get them engaged in an AdWords Account Audit & Strategy Session. In this session, one of my analysts studies and dissects their Google AdWords account with a fine-tooth comb. Is their keyword list holding back profits? Are they ignoring the biggest source of traffic that Google can provide? How do they have tracking set up – are they tracking the right or wrong metric for conversion? We look at their account structure – many times clients can realize a 20% or more improvement through structural reorganization.

If they're currently spending at least five thousand dollars per month on AdWords, we guarantee we will show them how to pocket the fee they pay to us for the Audit Session (and pocket it over and over again) by increasing their revenue from their campaigns – even if they don't end up signing on as a client.

Best of all, it's a low-cost, low-risk way for them to get a lot of great feedback on their account – and the money they pay us for this service (they can choose either a $1,000 or a more comprehensive $2,000 option) will get completely credited back to their account if they sign on with us within 21 days of their audit.

Should they want to continue on to management with us, we will assign them a dedicated PPC team led by a leader with a minimum of 6 years experience in PPC. That team leader will send a welcome letter introducing himself, their account manager and their analytics engineer. Also included will be a Jump Start Survey they fill out to give us an idea of what they want to accomplish through us.

We then have a Jump Start Call with our new client that lasts up to an hour in which we learn more about the client's objectives and goals. From there, we come up with an action plan for analytics implementation, account development and improvement - and we continue on from there.

BOOSTING THE BEGINNER

The second group of clients we help are beginners to PPC and AdWords campaigns. We offer these people a great deal of free online resources, including an ad writing guide, and a video explaining some AdWords strategies. We've also made available (for just the price of shipping and handling) a free tips booklet and DVD with 50 of our best AdWords strategies.

Beginners are also able to pay $97 to access a training course on our site. And by "beginners," we mean that we only assume that you know how to turn your computer on and open up your web browser. We show you the rest.

As I said, we are always out in front of the latest online trends – and our goal is always to enable our clients to make more money. That may involve having them spend more to make more – or it may involve showing them they can spend less and still make big profits.

More and more businesses are realizing the dramatic impact that the internet can have to help them scale and grow their business. In particular, growing companies know their PPC advertising could realize an improvement if only a team was dedicated to keeping on top of the account – they know they're losing money and need help.

We're here to help with your online advertising efforts no matter what stage you're in with your internet campaigns, from complete novice to seasoned veteran. There's a lot of money out there to be made – and we're happy to help you make it.

As we mentioned earlier, we've created a free booklet containing 50 of our most valuable AdWords strategies, and we'd like to share 10 of our favorite tactics with you. These are imperative to keep in mind no matter what type or level of PPC advertiser you are.

ROI Revolution's Top 10 Tactics To Make Your AdWords Advertising Drive More Response & More Profit

Tactic 1: Add negative keywords to cut your unwanted spending

- Negative keywords prevent your ads from showing in response to irrelevant search queries, save you money and put more advertising dollars back in your pocket.

Tactic 2: Organize your account's keywords in a logical manner

- Logical organization saves time and energy in the management and analysis of your account.
- With tighter ad groups, keyword lists can match the ad text better - which increases your quality score.

Tactic 3: Don't ever put Search and Content in the same campaign

- *Always* split Content Network traffic into its own campaign because the performance of Search and Content Network traffic can vary dramatically.
- Content Network requires a unique ad group structure and usually lower bids than Search Network traffic.
- Content Network ads cater to someone who wasn't actively searching for your product or service.

Tactic 4: Adjust bids for each match type depending on performance

- Broad, phrase, and exact matches perform differently – often a *broad match* keyword may need a lower bid than its *exact match* version.

Tactic 5: Strive to bid for the ad position that maximizes your ROI

- While having your ad in higher positions may yield more clicks and therefore more conversions than lower spots, it doesn't always ensure the best ROI.
- If you pay twice as much per click to get your ad to positions 1-3 but find that it only gets you a few more sales and ultimately cuts into your profits, consider bidding less.

Tactic 6: Check your placements often on the Content Network

- Managed: Placements that you have specifically targeted
- Automatic: All other placements where your ads are showing on the Content Network
- Adjusting the bids on specific websites based on performance is a great way to boost ROI.

Tactic 7: Avoid making changes to your account too often

- Too many changes make it difficult, if not impossible to track the impact of your changes.
- If you make a large change, such as a major round of bid adjustments:
- Give it a full week to collect data, then check the impact.
- If the impact was negative, make more adjustments and wait another week.

Tactic 8: Promote the benefits, not features, in your ad text

- Features
- Specific qualities about your product or service
- Example: "Fuel efficient 51 mpg"
- Benefits
- "What's in it for me?"
- Example: "Spend less money on gas"
- The benefits will speak to the searcher in a more personal way, and increase the likelihood that they'll click your ad and end up on your site.

Tactic 9: Always evenly test at least two ads in any given ad group

- Over time, one ad will have a higher click-through rate (CTR) than the other.
- A higher CTR increases quality score, lowers average cost-per-click, and enables your ad to show in a higher position without having to increase your bids.
- Once you find a winning ad, write another to try to beat the control.

Tactic 10: Keep an eye on the cost per conversion of ads in the same ad group

- The ad with the higher CTR might also have a much higher cost per conversion, potentially lowering the profitability of your account.
- Bottom line: Stick with the ad that makes you the most money.

To get all 50 AdWords strategies in a 16-page pocket guide booklet mailed to you free of charge, complete the form online at: www.roirevolution.com/roisecrets.

ABOUT TIMOTHY

Timothy Seward started a wholesale distribution company in the "bricks and mortar" world in the 1990's and successfully sold it freeing himself up for a new adventure.

Realizing that technology was the edge that allowed him to grow his successful business so quickly, he went back to school for a degree in computer science - and then he discovered the Internet.

In a few short years, Google discovered him and his web marketing company ROI Revolution. They made him a charter consulting partner for their Google Analytics and Google Website Optimizer as well as a Google AdWords Qualified Advertising Company.

Today, Timothy and his staff of twenty-three engineers and paid search analysts guide the Internet marketing efforts of dozens of companies large and small in all kinds of businesses.

If understanding Google and knowing how to track the numbers of your business are important to you, you won't find a more qualified advisor. Learn more about ROI Revolution at www.roirevolution.com/roiexperts.

CHAPTER 23
DYNAMIC TRACKING: MEASURING YOUR ONLINE ROI

by Richard Seppala, The ROI Guy

H i, "The ROI Guy" here again to talk to you about Dynamic Tracking. You might think that has something to do with a new Radial Tire feature or something, but no, it actually relates to Timothy Seward's awesome chapter that you hopefully just read.

Timothy's ROI Revolution company does an amazing job of helping clients optimize Google AdWords campaigns and track the results. Obviously, I think it's incredibly important to make sure you're getting the bang for your buck in your online marketing, and the only way to do that is through accurately measuring your response and conversion rates.

But what happens when your online marketing generates *offline* responses and conversions? Many people are much more comfortable picking up the phone and calling a business, especially if they have specific questions or just immediately want to book your product or service. And you obviously want to give them as many options to do business as possible – so you leave a phone number for prospects to call, in addition to the online 'opt-in' box.

That's where I come in with my ROI Guy Dynamic Tracking System. We can generate an incredible amount of information about what online mechanism generated that phone call and integrate it with your existing online metrics.

You want a complete picture of what's generating the most leads and the most profits for your company, so you can focus on the marketing that works - and save money by slashing placements that just don't deliver. That's what Dynamic Tracking helps you do.

CUSTOM NUMBERS CREATED AUTOMATICALLY

You're probably wondering how you can track, with phone numbers, just what online site or search engine generated a lead. Well, it's easy with Dynamic Tracking. Through Java script rewrite or your site proxy – or just plain magic, if you really don't want to deal with the mechanics! - the phone number that's displayed to your prospect *physically changes, depending on where the traffic is coming from.* That's right, a different phone number appears on the same website to different people.

For example, let's say I have a new marketing campaign out there (because I pretty much always do). Someone does a search on "ROI Guy" on Google, and that takes them to my website at: www.YourROIGuy.com. The number they see on the screen? Let's say it's 555-555-7000. Someone else clicks through a PPC ad for my services and also arrives at my website. The number *they* see is 555-555-0007 – because the phone number automatically changes since they came to my site from a different source.

And if the person already has my site bookmarked, as any smart marketer would, and goes directly to my website on their own, they'll see yet another number when they arrive – let's say it's 555-555-0707.

The same process works for a Yahoo! search, my Facebook page, a banner ad or just a different search engine set of keywords that takes the prospect to my site. All of these create *different trackable phone numbers on the same website* – and also generates the following data online for me to take a look at:

- Search engine keywords used to find my site, or:
- URL of website that referred them to mine
- Whether it was an organic search or a PPC link
- Time of call
- Phone number used
- Location of caller
- IP Address of caller
- Length of call

You can make use of as many phone numbers, or as few as, you like. You can just measure a specific campaign that may be spread across several online portals/ads or measure each individual ad/link. Customize it to what you consider the most useful information – and also create custom reports to put all the data together.

It's also useful to compare how much traffic and how many conversions you're getting, from organic searches versus paid online ads. Your Facebook Fan page may be doing more for you than a Google AdWords campaign, who knows??

Of course, you don't have to have fifty people sitting around with fifty different phones to answer those fifty phone numbers. All the phone numbers go to the same place you designate, whether it's your office or to an automatic answering system like my "ROI Bridge" package that works with Infusionsoft to automatically record and capture generated lead contact info. But the online data from each individual phone number is recorded online.

Best of all, as I mentioned earlier, you can integrate the ROI Guy Dynamic Tracking System results with a variety of existing web analytics such as Google Analytics, so the calls will show up alongside your online traffic data.

TRACKING TECHNOLOGY THAT DELIVERS

Again, just tracking your online responses only tells half the story. The phone is still the most efficient tool for prospects if they have immediate questions or want fast action. And, when used with an effective Call to Action and contact capture system, this also produces an awesome ROI.

Now that we have the technology that allows us to instantly rewrite phone numbers and display different ones to different online prospects, it gives us another essential tool we can use to monitor what internet placements and marketing are bringing the best results. I say "essential," because, as we all know, online behavior adapts and changes constantly on a day-to-day basis. Marketers and entrepreneurs need to continually analyze the latest trends and traffic patterns to put the most effective online campaign together.

With our Dynamic Tracking System, we can complete the picture of what's *really* driving online traffic and conversions – and we can update it on a daily basis. By staying on top of the changing world of the internet, you stay on top of your marketing game – enabling you to generate more leads, convert more leads to cash and maintain a dominant online presence.

Make sure you're not spending marketing money that's just disappearing down an online 'hole'. Make sure you're focusing on what's making you the most money. Compliment your online analytics with Dynamic Tracking of your offline phone calls and you'll position yourself for ongoing success.

ABOUT RICHARD

Your ROI Guy – Richard Seppala

Richard Seppala, a.k.a. Your ROI Guy, has spent years in direct sales and marketing and is now using his knowledge to help businesses across the nation. He has been referred to as the Call Tracking Expert, and has been featured on CBS, ABC, NBC and FOX, as well is in The Wall Street Journal. As the president of Total Census Solutions, Richard uses his extensive experience to help his clients with one of their biggest marketing dilemmas – knowing their marketing ROI.

How did Richard obtain such a deep understanding of ROI when it comes to marketing campaigns? He spent more than a decade as the vice president of sales and marketing for top providers within the long-term care industry. During that time, he developed unique and creative marketing programs that consistently surpassed census goals and financial satisfaction. He learned early on that the key to marketing success is knowing your numbers.

Richard now provides innovative programs and technologies to other businesses, to allow them to easily monitor, track and quantify the effectiveness of their marketing campaigns. He has also created systems that help companies improve upon their customer service and in-office presentations.

If you are ready to market with confidence, contact Your ROI Guy today!

CHAPTER 24
AUTOPILOT YOUR SMALL BUSINESS TO THE NEXT LEVEL!

by Dave Lee, VP Sales & Business Development,
Infusionsoft

W hat's the difference between success and failure in today's business world? Marketing, marketing, marketing.

Oh, and did we also mention "marketing?"

You can have the best product or service in the world and it might not mean a thing – unless you have the marketing machinery in place to sell it to the world.

But, you might say, you're a small business without the money to put that machinery in place. You don't have the time or the resources to really sell yourself effectively. You're already working 24/7 to keep things running as well as they are – and you still find yourself falling behind.

That's where Infusionsoft comes in. We've created marketing software designed *specifically for entrepreneurs and small businesses* that enables you to do effortless follow-up marketing campaigns with your prospects and customers. Our growth has been explosive – because our clients have achieved great success with the automatic systems we provide them with.

If they hadn't found that kind of success, we wouldn't have been able to start our legendary "Double Your Sales Club." Yes, it's for clients who have doubled their sales with the help of Infusionsoft. We wouldn't have started the club if we didn't have enough clients achieving amazing results – because there's nothing more depressing than starting a club that nobody qualifies for. Instead, we've got a very healthy membership that we'd like you to be a part of – but more on that later.

Elsewhere in this book, you've read - or will read - Richard Seppala's chapter about his product, "The Bridge," which integrates with our Infusionsoft program. The ROI Guy is a great partner of ours who's an expert on tracking marketing placements and feeding leads into our software. He knows – as do his clients - that working with us makes for a powerful one-two punch, because we can deliver the kind of marketing follow-up firepower that can put you on equal footing with the 'big boys'.

What we do is help you use your captured leads to follow up with targeted marketing that's automatic and seamless. That now extends beyond auto responders and marketing emails to postcards, direct mail campaigns, faxes and voice messages. We've gone the extra mile to create a multimedia system that enables you to market your business with ease.

On our website at Infusionsoft.com, you can see the incredibly-gratifying testimonials from our customers about how they've built incredible success stories with Infusionsoft - with some of our clients going from zero to multi-million dollar businesses in just one year. Yes, it's important to have the right product or service targeted at the right market – but, when you combine that with the power of Infusionsoft, you get your message to the right person at the right time to make the sale.

We call the service we offer "smart, automated communication" – and we've designed our packages and business coaching services to grow with you as you implement our integrated automatic marketing system: a system that allows you to automate your marketing so you can concentrate on your core business. You don't have to spend your days and nights on needless tedious data entry tasks, which allows you to devote time to more important endeavors – like working on that replica of Hoover Dam you're building out of toothpicks (which, unfortunately, we *can't* help you with, but we'd sure like to take a look when you're done).

HOW WE'VE GROWN – AND YOU CAN TOO

In 2006, we had our first user conference ever – in an upstairs room at our office. We had a staggering crowd of 35 in attendance. That's not quite a club with nobody in it, but it's perilously close.

This year, however? We had over 1500 users. In the last few years, our growth in all areas has been incredible – from hundreds of users to over 20,000. The number of our employees has grown from a couple dozen to over 140, and our product has become more powerful, more feature-packed and easier to use.

What's behind our awesome growth? Yes, we believe we offer a superior product targeted at the right market at just the right time. But it's not just that. A large part of our success is due to our partnerships with our clients – the entrepreneurs and small business people who have realized that the old ways of selling no longer work and the old ways of managing contacts don't work.

Selling door-to-door is obviously as outdated as the Pony Express, and if there's still a Rolodex on your desk, then you should consider opening a museum instead of running a business. The old ways took a lot of time and a lot of energy. Those are two things that are in scarily short supply in modern life.

If you do run your own business, your resources are probably strained to the limit just to keep it going day-to-day. How do you take it to the next level without having a complete nervous breakdown? How do you grow without growing broke?

There are two critical factors every entrepreneur needs to grow their business:

1. A Powerful Marketing Plan

Growth isn't about how big your office is or about how many employees you have. It's about how many customers and prospects you can market to. Especially existing customers, since it's easier to sell to some you've already sold to, rather than chasing down new leads that have no relationship to you.

2. A Fulfillment Plan

Adding more customers to your marketing mix is one thing; continuing to communicate and deliver to them is another. If you don't have a foolproof means of developing follow-up, you not only lose out on new customers, you can also damage your relationship with your existing customers.

Those are the two factors we specifically aimed to address with Infusionsoft, designed to be a huge component of enabling your business to "move on up." And our latest incarnation, as we said, does more than ever.

EMAIL MARKETING 2.0

Our Email Marketing 2.0 software package is the next generation of email marketing for small businesses. It enables you to send the right message to the right person at the right time automatically. Here's how it goes beyond our Email Marketing 1.0 product:

- **Email Marketing 2.0 is "smart"** in the way the Web 2.0 is smart. By combining a powerful customer database (CRM) that tracks interests and behaviors with email marketing, Infusionsoft users can send timely and relevant emails and other communications that match your customers' and prospects' needs.
- **Email Marketing 2.0 includes a powerful autopilot.** It automatically responds to customer behavior based on the users' preference – and it does so in a personalized way.
- **Email Marketing 2.0 goes beyond email** to allow marketers to intelligently and automatically send targeted direct mail, faxes and voice messages, meaning you can now use it for multimedia communication.

And an important thing to realize about Infusionsoft is that we're much more than an email marketing system. No, we're not trying to turn this into a

Ginsu Knife offer – but we do offer a complete small business growth suite that gives entrepreneurs the tools they need to grow *fast* – a suite that includes:

- Referral Management (affiliates)
- Opportunity Management (workflow automation)
- Automated Billing
- Shopping Cart
- Order Forms
- Calendar and Task Management

We hesitate to add "and more" – we're still concerned about the "Ginsu Knives" comparison - but there *is* more, including a "Double Your Sales Success Path" that incorporates our proprietary 9 Building Blocks Coaching Program that will help you automate and grow.

In other words, we don't just dump our stuff on you and do a vanishing act. We offer coaching programs that give you the training and account management resources you need to maximize the Infusionsoft advantage. We consider ourselves small business growth experts – because if we help our clients succeed, that helps us succeed. And that's why we consider ourselves partners with everyone who uses our services.

STARTING WITH INFUSIONSOFT

Hopefully, we haven't thrown too much at you in the last few pages. Again, we want to emphasize that we know how to work with small business – our average client has somewhere between 2 and 10 employees. But we want your small business to do big business and we do everything in our power to empower you towards that end.

That starts with our 15 day free trial, which you can take advantage of at: *www.infusionsoft.com/roi*. That gets you started with our basic package - you can add on some extra bells and whistles as you go along when you find it necessary. Our partnership with you continues with the fact that *you never sign a contract with us*. We go strictly month-to-month, and, if you're not happy with what we're delivering, you're free to stop using us.

A PROVEN SUCCESS PATH

Recently, we unveiled our "Double Your Sales" Success Path which each new customer gets on board with before we let them start using the software. It's a clear and simple roadmap or blueprint that outlines the critical things to ensure success with the software… and their business. Details of the Double Your Sales Success Path can be found on our website (www.infusionsoft.com), but the high-level roadmap includes:

- Send your first broadcast (2.0-style)
- Launch the "Key 3" campaigns (new lead, new customer, long term nurture)
- Automate & grow (by applying the 9 building blocks)
- Join the Double Your Sales Club

We understand how tough it is to run a growing business, so to make sure you stay on the path we assign a Success Coach to each new customer. The Success Coach acts like a personal trainer who makes sure you are using the right equipment, don't get distracted, and focus on activities that produce quick results. They make sure you progress along the path and get value out of the software. (Unlike a gym, we actually want you using your membership/subscription!)

So please take advantage of our 15 day free trial at: *www.infusionsoft.com/roi*. Also feel free to check out a free demo of just what Infusionsoft is all about at: http://www.infusionsoft.com, where you can also watch a product overview video, see all the nice words our great clients have to say about us, and get access to a wide range of free resources that will educate you both about growing your business and how to use Infusionsoft to help make that growth happen.

Marketing, marketing, marketing. It makes the biggest difference – but it's also where businesses stumble most of the time, because they just don't have the time and the technology to do it effectively. Infusionsoft is the affordable, cost-effective solution that makes cutting-edge marketing not only available but *easy* for any size business.

We look forward to having you join our Double Your Sales Club. Trust us, it's a very happy room to be in.

ABOUT DAVE

Dave Lee absolutely loves working with Infusionsoft as Vice President of Business Development. He is a veteran with web-based software (SaaS) and has been using the Internet since 1988 when he first logged on with a Prodigy account to check the Lake Tahoe ski report each night.

His prior decade working in technology & software companies combined with an entrepreneurial spirit, political science & MBA degrees, and his love of marketing, sales, & working with people make Dave a powerful contributor on the Infusionsoft executive team. Outside of work, Dave loves spending time with his family, lives to snow ski (watch one of Dave's ski adventures), and enjoys world travel and reading.

CHAPTER 25
HOW TO MAP OUT YOUR SUCCESS

by Darrin T. Mish, Esq.

Y ou know, it's pretty awesome when a new business finds you, instead of you having to find a new business.

Thanks to Google Maps, that's just what happened to me.

I'm primarily a tax attorney and my main practice is geared towards helping those with IRS problems. One of my passions, however, is also online marketing, and that means I put a lot of effort into giving my practice a large internet presence. It's helped me build my business from being merely local to national and even international in scope.

And now, online marketing has even given me a whole new law practice – bankruptcy protection. I had people calling my office and demanding that I should be providing this service. Seriously. Why would they do that, when it was nothing that I did provide?

Because Google Maps said I did, that's why. And as we all know, what Google says these days, goes!

Seriously, I'll explain just how it all happened at the end of this chapter. But first, I have to explain why Google Maps may be the best online marketing tool you're *not* using. And as I do explain, I'll be happy to provide driving directions that will lead you to your own success.

ESCAPING THE THICKEST PART
OF THE PHONE BOOK

When I was in college about 20 years ago, my roommate used to razz me about my wanting to become a lawyer. He said the attorneys were always in the thickest part of the yellow pages – meaning, I would just get lost in the shuffle. There were already too many lawyers.

Well, he was right – about lawyers being the thickest part of the phone book. I checked it out myself and you should feel free to take a look too - if you can actually find a phone book to do it with, of course. They're kind of hard to find these days.

Because what my roommate *didn't* see was that, two decades later, the phone book would be heading the way of the dinosaur. Studies show that people under 40 to 45 don't even use the phone books anymore – they look everything up online. Meanwhile, Yellow Pages ads get more and more expensive – and less and less effective.

But my roommate's words stuck with me – I knew marketing my law firm would need to be a vital part of my success. So when online marketing became a viable vehicle to advertise and differentiate a business, I jumped on the new technology to promote my practice and my services to the entire internet community.

Using SEO (Search Engine Optimization) really made a huge impact – when your law practice ends up being ranked high in the Google search results, it makes success almost a guarantee. And, as I said earlier, this meant my business went from being just a local law practice to one that's currently being used by people all over the world.

Best of all? Most online marketing methods are absolutely free. And the one I'm going to talk about in this chapter, Google Maps, is no exception. There is only one paid service I am going to recommend (it will cost you a whopping $30 a year) but even that one isn't necessary.

Now, let's map out the way you can use Google Maps to reach people at just the exact right moment you want to reach them – *when they're ready to buy.*

MAP MAGIC

To begin with, let me say upfront that I'm only going to discuss this in terms of Google Maps – what I'm going to describe, however, works just as effectively (and similarly) with Yahoo! and Bing Maps. Google, however, delivers an incredibly higher amount of traffic, so their maps service is what I'm going to focus on.

You can make Google Maps work for you, no matter what business you're in, as long as you're listed with Google Maps as a local provider. People go to: www.maps.google.com when they're looking for something. They're not just looking for names of places, though – they're also looking for *people and businesses.* And when they're looking for the kind of business you're in, you want them to find *you.*

When consumers are using Google Maps to find a business, that means they're at a pretty serious stage. They're probably in need of someone at that moment and don't know who to turn to. In other words, you have the opportunity to reach them at the precise moment every marketer craves a shot at – the moment when they're ready to open their wallet and pay for your product or service.

Getting yourself at the top of that Google Maps search results page gives you a huge advantage in making that moment count for the most. Generally speaking, if you get yourself at the top of the results, you'll get four times as many click-throughs as the next company down on the list. That's a massive amount of traffic you can have coming your way just by taking the proper steps.

For example, if you put "Tampa tax attorney" into the Google Maps search engine, here's what you'll see:

Yes, you'll see half of my head on the left (I'll have to look into that…). But you'll also notice my law firm is at the very top of the results – linked to the letter "A," which marks my office location on the actual map. All the vital information is there, and it's more detailed than any of the other companies in the results column.

How did I get that awesome placement? More importantly, how can you get that kind of placement for *your* business? Read on!

CREATING YOUR MAP PROFILE

As is often the case with internet marketing, the key is *keywords*. Keywords, which are the words or phrases people use to search for things through search engines such as Google, are crucially important to optimizing your Google Maps results position.

Keep in mind that there are two kinds of keywords in this arena – "research" keywords and "buy" keywords. For example, in my niche, "tax law" is a research keyword phrase, mostly used by people who want more information on the laws and possibly aren't ready to hire an attorney yet. That's not so important for Google Maps. For a buy keyword phrase, "Tampa tax attorney" is perfect – it's not as competitive as only "tax attorney" and obviously it pinpoints my location for people in the area.

It's hard for me to advise you exactly on what keywords will work for your business, but there is an excellent free Google tool at: https://adwords. google.com/select/KeywordToolExternal. You'll want to try and find keywords for your business that have monthly searches of over 1000. And since Google

Maps allows you to list five categories for your business, you'll want to find five of those keyword phrases. Again, putting in your locality will help your results.

By the way, if your business has more than one location, you can do separate listings on Google Maps. Also, if your business has *no* location (i.e. you work out of your home or, say, you're a plumber who works off your cell phone number), Google permits you to rent a mailbox location and use that as your physical address. If you do that, get your mailbox as close to the middle of the town or city you're located in – the closer to the center you are, the higher your ranking will be.

Next, with keywords in hand, you'll want to create your Google Map business listing. Go to: www.google.com/localbusinesscenter and sign in with your gmail account (which is easy to create if you don't have one). Click on the "Add New Business" button in the upper right of the screen and get started!

Some simple tips and tricks:

- **Fill out the form as completely as possible** – the more information you give, the higher Google will rank you.
- **Be as consistent as possible**. Always spell out your business name **the exact same way** (choose either Inc. or Incorporated, for example) and your address the exact same way (choose either W. Main Street or West Main Street, for example).
- **Use the same phone number** in all your info.
- **Use a special email address**, not your normal one, because you're bound to get spammed a lot as a result of this listing.
- When you put in your website address, **make sure it's a fully-resolved URL** so anyone can click through on it.
- **Make sure your keywords appear in your business description**. Make the description sales-oriented, but not too much so. People want a legitimate business, not an advertisement. Remember, they're after information here and you have a limited amount of space to provide it.
- You can **enter up to five categories**. Use them all and **use your top keywords** in them. You can choose the wording of at least four of their categories – one of them has to already be in their already-approved business category list.
- You can **upload up to ten photos**. It helps if you upload as many as you can.
- Name your photo files with your top keywords. For example, mine are tampataxattorney1.jpg, tampataxattorney2.jpg, etc. Believe it or not, this also helps your Google Maps ranking.
- **Include photos of the exterior of your building** if you can, so people can recognize it if they're coming to your place of business.
- You can **include a coupon** on your listing – and you should do it. Check out the one on my listing for an example – many businesses do this.

- **Add videos if you can** – you have room to add five from YouTube, you just have to paste the YouTube URL in the designated space. If you don't have videos and want an easy way to create some slick-looking ones, check out: www.animoto.com – they'll create :30 second highly-produced slideshow videos for free (if you need more photos for the videos, you can buy some cheaply at: www.istockphoto.com).

Again, *the more information you provide in your Google Maps listing, the better your ranking will be.* Take advantage of that fact and pack as much in as possible.

OTHER WAYS TO RAISE YOUR RANKING

In addition to packing your listing with as much consistent information as you can, there are two other factors that contribute to giving you a top Google Maps ranking.

- **Reviews**

If you go back to Google Maps and search on "Tampa Tax Attorney," you'll again notice my law firm ranks at the top of the list. I also want you to notice I have 9 reviews from clients on my listing. Now, the first review I received was less-than-flattering – fortunately, the next eight were great and buried its impact.

Now check out the next couple of lawyers listed after me - you'll see they have *no* reviews.

Reviews help your ranking. Obviously, you want to have good ones, because you're pretty much stuck with them once you get them. My suggestion is to ask clients you're comfortable with to give you an online review and give them some kind of incentive – a discount or bonus of some sort. *Do not ask them specifically to write a good review* – that's not cool. If they're happy clients, you can be pretty sure they will give you a positive write-up. Just tell them to write whatever they want.

Also, *avoid writing your own good reviews.* Yes, it's tempting, but Google can usually tell and you'll get in a whole bunch of trouble you don't need.

- **Citations**

Google also uses citations to determine your organic ranking – these are the number of links on other sites that point back to your site. Google spiders are constantly out there looking for instances of businesses being legit and real. Having other highly-rated sites acknowledging and linking back to you gives your search engine sizzle that extends to Google Maps.

Here are a few more sites where you can list your business details for free and that Google will look kindly on:

www.YellowPages.com
www.InfoUSA.com

www.localeze.com
www.Supermedia.com
www.NAVTEQ.com

Now, remember when I mentioned that I would only recommend one service that you actually had to pay for? You'll find that service at: www.UniversalBusinessListing.org. There, for a $30 annual fee, they will put your business details everywhere on not only internet directories, search engines, guides and portals, but also on cell phone directories and GPS systems. I think it's an incredible way to get your business posted everywhere, it saves you a lot of time and, to me, it's worth the price.

If you haven't already put in the time to create your Google Maps listing, I suggest you do so as soon as you can. It can take anywhere from two to three months for your listing to hit the top of the Google Maps results rankings. Remember that you can edit your listing at any time after you create it, so don't worry about getting something wrong temporarily – it's more important that you just get it done.

If you are in a big city and in a competitive field, it may take a lot of work to hit the top. And you may want to hire a professional to do it. One place to find someone to handle it for you is on: www.elance.com, where you'll find lots of online marketing pros who will bid against each other to do the job. We would also be happy to take on the task at my company: www.LocalTrafficExplosion.com, so contact us for more information – we even guarantee you don't have to pay if you don't reach your desired spot.

How effective was Google Maps for my law firm? As I mentioned at the beginning of this chapter, we expanded into a whole new legal business because of them. What happened was, because we ranked so high on Google Maps as tax lawyers, we suddenly started showing up in the results for "bankruptcy attorney" – even though we didn't handle bankruptcy!

We had no idea this was going on, until we began getting phone calls from people asking us about bankruptcies. When we told them that bankruptcy wasn't part of the services we offered, some of them actually got *angry* at us – because they thought we were doing false advertising!

Well, seeing the opportunity, we opened a new law firm specializing in bankruptcies. If you can't beat 'em, join 'em, I always say – and, thanks to Google Maps, I have added a whole new layer of success to my business.

So map out a path for your success with Google and all the other online map services. It's the perfect moment to use this underutilized but incredibly effective (and free!) online marketing tool.

The world can be right at your doorstep – if you let Google Maps direct it there!

ABOUT DARRIN

Darrin T. Mish, Esq. is an attorney with two very successful law practices located in the Tampa, Florida area. He has been able to grow both of these separate practices into extremely profitable ventures without losing time for the things that are important in life such as family, recreation time and hobbies. He is a master in the internet traffic generation, search engine optimization and Google Maps in particular. His unique 'out of the box' thinking, coupled with his desire to completely DOMINATE markets is why you should listen to him. His methods will have your small business swamped with customers. He can be reached at his website at: http://localbusinessexplosion.com

CHAPTER 26
DIRECT MAIL: WHAT'S THE LATEST, GREATEST THING WE CAN DO?

by Tony Wedel, General Manager,
McMannis Duplication and Fulfillment

D irect Mail can be one of the most creative, impactful tools a marketer can use. Even in this day and age, when online marketing is the hot topic, there are certain things you can do with Direct Mail that you just cannot match in other mediums where you cannot actually feel or touch anything.

Like, for example, the time we sent out dirty diapers to our customer's mailing list.

Okay, they weren't really dirty diapers – they were actually clean diapers, we just placed Tootsie Rolls inside them. It was a direct mail piece aimed at retail outlets with the message, "Don't let your customers crap all over you." I'm cleaning up the language a little, but you get the idea.

You get something like that in the mail, you don't forget it.

I'm certainly not going to say a pretend-dirty diaper is the best way to go with a Direct Mail campaign, but I can say that we've sent all sorts of fun giveaways – everything from candy to cold, hard cash – inside our clients' direct mail pieces. These kinds of attention-getters bring a smile and make people want to open it up to find out more.

An email you can just click on and delete without ever reading cannot compete with the physical impact of the packages we send out – and that's a big advantage you cannot ignore in an overcrowded marketing environment.

That's why, when we consult with clients, we always ask, "What's the latest, greatest thing we can do?" Then we make it happen.

WHY DIRECT MAIL IS A BIG DEAL

American marketers have always found the mail to be an amazing way to get their message across, ever since this country began. William Penn in the 1700's did the first "mailers" in America for a land ownership business – while you could say Benjamin Franklin did the first "newsletter" with Poor Richard's Almanac.

At its best, Direct Mail can be a really creative and fun way to deliver your message and keep up with your mailing list. The fact is, that message can easily get lost in an overcrowded email box these days. While many people think Direct Mail is going the way of the dinosaur and the fax machine, the truth is that, because less and less is actually mailed to people anymore, Direct Mail stands out more than ever in a mailbox.

Research shows Direct Mail has a great ROI – it generates more responses than email, magazine, newspaper and radio ads, so it more than justifies its cost. An article, "Firms Hold Fast to Snail Mail Marketing," about Direct Mail in "The Wall Street Journal" from January 12th, 2010, tells the story of Alicia Settle, President of a New York company, Per Annum. She decided that the $20,000 a year she spent on Direct Mail was a waste – so she cut that amount from her company's budget and instead concentrated on email marketing.

And she saw a 25% drop in orders.

"We realized we had made a huge mistake," is how she's quoted in the article.

Other executives discuss in the same article how they build up customer loyalty – and, in one case, generated $270,000 in new business - because they used Direct Mail effectively. Incidentally, that $270,000 came from a $4,000 mailing – a good ROI in anybody's book!

ONE-STOP SHOPPING

What's important when it comes to Direct Mail is to deal with a company that can do everything from A to Z. Otherwise, you can end up with three or four different vendors going in three or four different directions.

Our company, McMannis Duplication and Fulfillment (www.mcmannisinc.com), started off 9 years ago as a part-time venture – we bought a cassette tape-duplication business and, for a while, that's all we did – copy cassettes. Obviously, we had to add CDs and DVDs into the mix to continue to be competitive.

What we also saw, however, was a lot of customers went one place to get their printing done, one place to get their tapes and discs duplicated, and another place to get the whole package put together and mailed out. Nobody talked to one another, unfortunately, and a lot of problems came out of that fragmented system.

That's why we decided to create a start-to-finish service at McMannis that made it easy for all of our clients, big and small, to seamlessly get their Direct Mail campaigns out the door the way they want it …when they want it. Our customers liked it a lot better and so did we, as we finally got to see projects all the way through. When there are other vendors involved, we coordinate the whole project.

We were also in a better position, once we began to do the complete Direct Mail process for people, to advise and consult clients on their individual campaigns and offer cost-cutting and creative suggestions to do them effectively and efficiently.

The best example of how we've grown alongside our customers is a businesswoman in California who was just starting out with her marketing 3 years ago. Her first job that she gave us was duplication services on a few CDs. She took the principles of great marketing, applied them to differentiate herself, and has now gotten to the point where she has 32 different product lines, produces webinars and video seminars that she puts on discs and offers them as an up sell, and has 450 people who pay to subscribe to her newsletter. She also markets regularly to tens of thousands of people in her niche market. We were happy that our services helped her to build to this incredible success.

THE GLAZER-KENNEDY CONNECTION

This particular businesswoman learned her expertise from the master marketers, Bill Glazer and Dan Kennedy, who use us regularly for many of their duplication services, ordering anywhere from 20 copies of 'something' to 20,000 copies. We enjoy working with Glazer-Kennedy Insider's Circle (GKIC) members, and we currently are lucky enough to count around 250 of them as our regular customers.

When you're doing a Direct Mail campaign or shipping your products, you want a fulfillment house that understands the 'ins-and-outs' of marketing. Because we work with so many expert marketers, we know the drill. You want to deliver a consistent message in an impressive way so you rise above the pack and stand out from everyone else. We want to help you make that happen.

That's our mindset from the beginning with any client – how do we make your campaign unique and exciting? Since we do our own printing, we can create your own newspaper article or magazine tear-out for your campaign – and our staff will even handwrite with a Sharpie on those created articles and make it look like you personally wrote your own message to the person we are mailing out the article to (we can even make that handwriting sloppy or neat, depending on your preference!).

We also specialize in what's called "Shock and Awe" packages, which, as those of you who are GKIC members know, is a box of materials that's designed to dazzle customers with the sender's expertise and experience.

Because we do the entire Direct Mail process for our clients, a multistep campaign is also easier to pull off, since we can take care of each step of a drip campaign onsite. From the big packages to the little unique postcard reminders, we know how to get it done.

We want you to focus on the marketing and the overall "big idea", and let McMannis worry about all of the little details. We help clients choose the right kind of envelopes – a specific color or a metallic glamour envelope – and we offer ideas on how the envelope should be addressed, even on how the stamp should be placed on it.

Printing challenges are also our specialty. We had one client that wanted to send out a 12 page sales booklet with a CD – and wanted to avoid a higher postal rate by keeping the envelope letter-sized and under the 6" x 11.5" limit. At the same time, we had to make sure the CD didn't move around inside the booklet and possibly get broken going through the Post Office machinery.

The solution was to saddle-stitch a 6" x 9" booklet inside a card stock cover – and do a special die-cut inside back cover to insert the CD. The CD stayed put and the mailing was a big success.

When you call a Direct Mail house, you want to be confident that when you say you want something unique and memorable, the people there can help you make it happen. We have so much experience with so many different types of clients that we're always aware of the hottest designs and gimmicks going on at the moment – and can also access great campaigns we've helped create in the past (without violating any client's confidentiality or using the same idea for a competing business).

Our objective is always to make sure the mailing gets opened and not thrown away. And we give every customer the same kind of personal attention, whether they're having a few copies of a CD made or doing a huge multistep campaign.

For marketers willing to put in the time to make sure their Direct Mail piece is creative and exciting, the pay-off is always going to be there – and the ROI will be sky-high!

ABOUT TONY

What started out as a small sideline cassette duplicating business for one customer quickly grew when Jeff and Chris McMannis, owners of McMannis Duplication and Fulfillment, hired Tony Wedel to take their business to the next level.

Tony Wedel, General Manager of McMannis Duplication and Fulfillment, implemented an extensive plan of rapid growth and expansion. Utilizing his experience as a Corporate Manager for one of the largest privately held companies in the world, he has guided McMannis Duplication and Fulfillment, Inc. and developed it to what it is today. Over the last 10 years, the business has grown to over 175 customers in 5 countries.

Tony has introduced several services in addition to media duplication services that initially founded the company. These additional services include direct mail, product fulfillment, full service printing, special customization, lumpy mail and other related services

Tony is clearly the expert when it comes to understanding business philosophy and marketing his own business. And, with over 175 customers, he has the unique opportunity to see what other leading edge marketers are doing in their businesses.

If you are looking for a company to deliver the tangibles in your marketing funnel, contact Tony and the great staff at McMannis Duplication and Fulfillment, Inc.

CHAPTER 27
VIRTUAL ASSISTANTS CAN DO ALL THAT WORK THAT NO ONE HAS TIME TO DO

by Connie Gray

I t is 'way too easy' to get bogged down with the day-to-day activities involved in running your business. Many business owners and professionals find themselves filling their days with administrative work, instead of generating more business and increasing their bottom line. Even though doing data entry, creating spreadsheets or performing some bookkeeping tasks can quickly steal the day away, some business professionals are hesitant to hire help, out of concern about how much it will cost to add an employee or the commitment involved.

THERE IS A SOLUTION!

As telecommunications have made it easier for people to work together from all over the world, it has also opened up a great opportunity for companies that need help, but don't want to commit to hiring new staff. If your business falls into this group, then you need to become familiar with *Virtual Assistants*.

DEFINITION & HISTORY OF VIRTUAL ASSISTANTS

The Virtual Assistance Chamber of Commerce defines a Virtual Assistant as:

A Virtual Assistant (or VA) is a solopreneur who specializes in providing ongoing, one-on-one, collaborative-style administrative support.
Like other professional service providers, Virtual Assistants operate remotely from their own places of business and utilize today's technology to deliver their services and communicate with clients.
Virtual Assistants are first and foremost administrative experts. Virtual Assistants sometimes offer additional, separate specialties that fall under creative and/or technical services.

191

Virtual Assistants come from a variety of business backgrounds, but the single-most important qualification the industry expects of its peers is at least five (5) years administrative experience earned in the real (non-virtual) business world working in upper-level capacities such as administrative assistant, executive assistant, secretary, legal assistant, paralegal, legal secretary, real estate assistant, office manager/supervisor, etc.

From this level of experience, a Virtual Assistant is expected to possess skill sets, training and business knowledge, which are the hallmark of a truly qualified Virtual Assistant.

A Virtual Assistant is someone who offers administrative support services, although many of them offer more types of services over the telephone and Internet. This person can help you take care of all the details of your business for you, even those things on your "to-do" list that you never seem to get to. Think of your Virtual Assistant as an executive assistant or office manager, but one who does not work in your office.

While the term "Virtual Assistant" may be relatively new, this profession began its evolution all the way back in the 1950s during the advent of secretarial services. In the early 1990s, as it started getting easier to work from remote locations, Virtual Assistants began stepping into the business realm. The virtual assistance industry has progressed significantly over recent years. According to VAnetworking.com, nowadays, a Virtual Assistant can become "your right hand person helping you succeed in your business. The irony is that you may never meet your Virtual Assistant as odds are they live nowhere near you!"

WORKING WITH A VIRTUAL ASSISTANT BENEFITS YOU

If you are a solo practitioner or small business owner, you might not have the time, space, budget or a big enough workload to justify hiring a full-time or even part-time person to come into the office. Having a Virtual Assistant is a great alternative to hiring someone in-house, plus there are many benefits that this person can offer. Below is just a sample of how a Virtual Assistant can help you:

1. ***They can do the work you never get to.*** Let's face it - there just isn't enough time in the day to get around to doing all of the "stuff" necessary to run your business and life. It's easy to 'push projects off' until the following day, but the truth is - you end up doing the same thing every day. The next thing you know, you have projects and tasks that never get completed. A Virtual Assistant can help you get all your projects finished in a timely manner.

2. ***They are someone to brainstorm with.*** A Virtual Assistant can gener-

ally provide you with more than just administrative support, and can become someone with whom you can bounce around ideas. Wouldn't it be nice to have someone who understands your vision and can help you get there?

3. *They can provide you with the chance to focus on what makes money.* You need to be able to spend your time and efforts on your main income-generating activities. A Virtual Assistant gives you the ability to reallocate your energy and focus, without having to worry that your day-to-day work is not being done.

4. *They can free up your time to spend doing the things you enjoy.* Wouldn't it be nice to have someone else taking care of the administrative details that steal your time? It would be great to have someone who can create your spreadsheets, keep your calendar and even plan your events. You can free up your time, so that you can be with your family more, go on that vacation or just have an uninterrupted lunch.

5. *They can protect your cash flow.* When you hire a Virtual Assistant, you are working with an independent contractor, not an employee. That means you won't incur some of the expenses associated with an employee, such as health benefits and overhead costs. However, you will still receive the help you need, just at a more reasonable cost. Plus, Virtual Assistants tend to be more experienced and efficient, so an employee's average 8 hour day, can be condensed into 3 to 4 hours with a Virtual Assistant.

A VIRTUAL ASSISTANT MAKES SENSE – JUST LOOK AT THE NUMBERS

When you compare the costs of hiring an employee versus a Virtual Assistant, working with a Virtual Assistant makes economical sense. Take a look at the following comparison:

COST COMPARISON	Full-time Employee	Virtual Assistant
Hourly Rate of Pay	$20.00	$35.00
Fringe Benefits @ 35% *(Health/Dental/Life Insurance, Retirement Plans)*		
	$7.00	None
Overhead Rate @ 50% *(Office Space, Equipment & Office Supply expense, UI Insurance, Worker's Compensation, Overtime Pay, Administration Costs)*		
	$10.00	None
Total Effective Rate of Pay	$37.00	$35.00
**Hours Per Year	2,080 hrs.	480 hrs.
TOTAL Annual Labor Cost	**$76,960.00**	**$16,800.00**

(Source: VAnetworking.com)

You really do not have a whole lot to lose by trying out a Virtual Assistant, but instead, you have a lot to gain. After you have read this book, there is no question that you will need assistance implementing all of the business ideas and strategies. A Virtual Assistant will be able to put it all together for you, to not only get your business on-track and 'on the road to success', but to help you take control of your time and life.

ABOUT VIRTUAL SOLUTIONS 4 YOU, LLC

Virtual Solutions 4 You, LLC offers a wide range of virtual services to businesses. As our client, we will help you handle your administrative duties online. Some of our offerings include general office support, proofreading and editing, website proofreading, telephone calling services, document or manuscript typing and handwritten services. At Virtual Solutions 4 You, LLC we focus not only on administrative duties, but also offer office or personal assistance.
Our trained professional staff is able to handle any task you can assign us. Our added advantage is that we have been working in the "Dan Kennedy" realm for two years, and we are very familiar with marketing for small businesses. Our staff is trained in InfusionSoft as well as a host of other software programs to help you.

Whether you need help with your routine operating duties or just need assistance with your busy life, Virtual Solutions 4 You, LLC is your answer. You can find us on the web at: www.virtualsolutions4you.com. Call us today at (913) 608-5346 to get your own Virtual Assistant working with you today!

ABOUT CONNIE

Connie Gray is the owner of Virtual Solutions 4 You. She possesses more than 27 years of experience in a wide range of education and administrative roles. Connie's background includes administrative support, education, grants, professional development, training and consulting. Her diverse knowledge allows her to bring new and innovative ideas to the table. She has been able to provide highly beneficial consulting services to many types of businesses and organizations.

Connie works closely with businesses to assist them with developing effective implementation plans.

When working with Connie, you can feel confident knowing you are partnering with a professional who will be honest and reliable. She prides herself on being upfront with her clients and keeps all information confidential.

CHAPTER 28
GET OUT OF YOUR AREA CODE

by Steven Placey, Founder, Rock Your Business™ Inc.

You want to take your business to new heights? Well, the best way to increase your ROI is to RYB – Rock Your Business!

Yes, that does happen to be the name of *my* business – but it's also my business philosophy. Look, you can read as many books like this as you want, but just reading isn't going to get the job done – even though I truly believe most of them are filled with great advice. I certainly wouldn't participate in this one if I didn't feel it was a worthwhile endeavor.

But if you ask me, what should business people do? Hey, that's simple. **They should *do***. Activity breeds activity – and too many entrepreneurs spend too much time thinking about what they *need* to do rather than actually *doing it*. And too many times they don't put into action that great advice they read all the time.

So let's get down to it – and talk about how to rock *your* business. And I want to do that by looking at one Jersey guy who rocked his business like no one else I've ever seen.

FROM 5 MILLION TO 60 MILLION

Probably many of you have heard of Gary Vaynerchuk – he's been profiled in "The New York Times," and on CBS and ABC news, he's appeared on the Conan O'Brien and Ellen Degeneres shows and has become a national figure. If you don't already know his story, you need to. Because this is a guy who took his parents' retail wine business to unimaginable heights.

The center of that business was the brick-and-mortar store, Shoppers' Discount Liquor, located in Central New Jersey. His Russian immigrant parents built that retail center until it was grossing close to 5 million a year. Not too shabby for a mom-and-pop operation.

But Gary thought he could do even better with it – a lot better - and create his own unbeatable personal brand at the same time. He trained himself in wine-tasting, became an expert and began advising customers on what was a good buy. He rebranded the store as "Wine Library." And he began increasing the store traffic and sales because people sought out his advice and liked his reboot of the business.

Gary had to face the facts, however – there was only so far you could take a retail wine store in New Jersey. And that's when he took the giant leap – the kind of giant leap so many of us are often afraid to take – that vaulted him into national prominence.

He thought beyond the walls of his family's store, started selling wine on-line and – most importantly - began recording a video wine blog, called Wineli-brary TV in 2006. By taking advantage of the boom in social media, he promoted the video blog and his website endlessly, through YouTube, Facebook and Twitter, until he got Wine Library to the point where sales had increased to 60 million a year – over ten times what it had been making. He also built his online presence to the point where, today, he has close to 90,000 visitors to his website on a daily basis, as well as 900,000 followers on Twitter.

Not only that, but Gary also turned himself into an incredibly successful self-help and business advice guru! He just signed a seven figure deal with a publishing house for a series of books and is amazingly in demand at business events all across the country.

ACTION LED TO SUCCESS

How did Gary pull all this off? I don't know for certain whether he read any self-help books, but I kind of feel he did everything step by step relying on his gut. He basically took a usual kids' job - working the cash register at his parents' store – and parlayed it into an astounding success story. And these are the steps that led him to this:

1. He Became An Authority

Gary claims he did not engage in any underage drinking – but, as a teen-ager, he did extensive taste testing of the elements that went into wine. When he did become legal, he had amassed enough of a palate so he could instantly tell what wines were wonderful – and which tasted like dirty laundry. He felt confi-dent to begin sharing his opinions with customers, even to the point of bashing some of the labels his store carried. The customers responded, because…

2. He Was Unconventional

Part of the reason Gary is so popular is because he totally went 'against the grain'. He didn't study at the feet of established wine experts who talk with great eloquence and don't click with regular consumers. Gary's in-your-face, tell-it-like-it-is attitude was refreshing, relatable and actually expanded the mar-ket for wine, because people who thought the world of wine was beyond them, suddenly found someone who talked their language.

3. He Thought Out Of The Box

Even though his parents had established what was, by any standards, a perfectly successful small business, Gary saw that it could be bigger and better. "Shoppers' Discount Liquor" was never going to be an inspiring brand – "Wine Library" could be.

4. He Went Beyond The Walls

Gary also took the business – and himself online. He didn't allow himself to be defined by one store location in New Jersey – he put himself and his business out there to the international internet community and sold both to everyone he could. Instead of only "The Garden State" being his marketplace, suddenly the whole world was.

5. He Built Beyond His Business

Using Wine Library as a base, Gary V. has also created a whole business around himself and his method of building a brand. He's now running his own marketing agency, with the help of his younger brother, as well as publishing books, speaking at events and, of course, still doing his wine video blog.

MAKE IT HAPPEN WITH *YOUR* BUSINESS

How did that headline over this section make you feel – "Make It Happen with *Your* Business." Did you feel excited and motivated? Or did you feel scared and did it make you want to crawl back into bed?

You can laugh if you want, but, believe it or not, we have a lot of clients who seem frightened of success – I have to seriously tell them, "You know what? *It's okay to make money.*"

These people actually get concerned about becoming too big and not being able to handle the extra work – well, then, you hire the people you need, I mean, take a look around, many out there could *use* a job.

Or, more importantly, business people worry about trying and *failing*. Well, it's just as okay to fail as it is to succeed. It means you tried – and you probably learned a few important lessons that will let you succeed next time. Staying stuck where you are? To me, that's failing.

At Rock Your Business™, we are about, as our tagline states, "Innovation and Solutions Today…for Your Company's Tomorrow." We're all about finding practical answers you can implement immediately to start building to a better business future. We do this both through one-on-one consulting, and also through our Rock Your Business™ America Clubs, where we gather up to 30 successful business owners and CEOS in a monthly meeting that serves as a "Think Tank" to provide positive, active methods to growing a business in today's tough economic climate. We also provide opportunities to put businesses at events where they can directly address anywhere from one hundred to one thousand people and expand their circle of influence.

In all of these energetic environments, we tackle such subjects as using social media, building strategic partnerships and engaging in affiliate programs to widen the reach and the impact of any business. And again, we focus on real-world, practical methodologies that are also exciting and impactful.

THE WORLD IS YOUR CUSTOMER

I frankly don't believe in limiting business to local customers anymore - that's why the title of this chapter is "Get Out of Your Area Code." Unless you do something like repair refrigerators, there's no reason you can't take who you are and what you do global, like Gary did. Putting your marketing budget into the community chamber of commerce just isn't a smart idea anymore – or very cost-effective.

Speaking for myself, I began my own video blog 22 weeks ago – TGIM (Thank God It's Monday). The link to that email gets sent out to 22,000 people every Monday morning – I look at it as an online jolt of caffeine to inspire and motivate my circle of business associates at the beginning of their work week (feel free to check it out at: http://rockyourbusinessnow.com/TGIM_Video_Blog_MEVU.html). When I did start it, it brought me $30,000 in extra profits – all for the cost of an hour of my time and the video camera. Now *that's* cost-effective.

Just as importantly, when I am at a business event, I'm recognized from that video blog. That means some people at a business event I may never have networked with will approach me, because they recognize me from my videos. It creates an immediate comfort level that's a giant assist when it comes to be-ginning a new and potentially profitable new relationship.

Gary inspired me to do that – and one big tip I will give to you in this chapter is that, if you see someone making money in a certain way, try that way too, if you have the resources to do it. What works for others will work for you – and, with the massive amount of internet marketing going on today, you have plenty of opportunity to study the tactics of those who are making good on a consistent basis.

It just makes sense to make your product or service available to anyone you can. If you can sell entry to a webinar for $50 to a hundred people, it's just as good as selling a one-on-one session for $500 to one person, with no real change to your workload or costs.

MAXIMIZE WHAT YOU HAVE

There's no better way to increase the ROI of your business than to use the resources and the talents you have available – that's also what all of us at Rock Your Business™ encourage. We work with businesses all the time and advise them to take their existing products/services and turn 'em, twist 'em and creatively work with them to make them more appealing or more profitable. We see if we can partner them up with other companies that complement their business, and we are also straight up about even eliminating some aspects of a product line that are just weighing a company down.

Creatively digging into your business model can always yield some nuggets of gold, especially if you can find a way to add your own passion to the mix. One business owner I work with sells promotional items. He's young, into surfing and skateboarding and he was getting a little burnt out on selling personalized pins, pens and those kinds of trinkets.

My thought was he needed to key a little more into who he was and use that to propel his business forward. I remembered how The RonJon Surf Shop built itself into a cool, hip brand that people all over the world are after – so I asked him if there were other surf or skateboard stores that he made shirts for and personalized with the store's logo. He said, yes, there were. I advised him to create his own line of clothes with an awesome design that would be *his* brand – but that could still be personalized with the stores' logos. That way they become the distributor of his brand – and it's more of a partnership rather than a straight sale. He thought that was a terrific idea and he's putting that plan into action.

By bringing your flavor, your interests and your energy to whatever you do, you not only better your chances of success, but you also feel more excited to work at it – because it's something that's now a part of you. Your personality needs to be the engine behind whatever you're doing – you don't need to be the smartest person, or the best-looking person, just be who you are and find the best way to express that with your business.

Take that energy and share it with the world, just as Gary did and just as I try to do with all of my clients. Activity generates activity – so think beyond whatever limits you're putting on yourself and give a new plan a try. You'll be rocking your business in no time at all!

ABOUT STEVEN

Steven Placey is known as a "Business PlayMaker" for his role in helping companies innovate new products, capitalize on their experiences and create new profit centers.

Steven founded Rock Your Business Club America - an Executive Think Tank and Innovation Forum exclusively for Business Owners and CEO's of Established and Emerging Companies.

Steven has helped thousands of Professionals to kick-start their innovation engines, energize their minds, and motivate them to go Rock their businesses - NOW!

Steven has been seen on ABC, CNN, MSNBC, CNBC. He has had articles published in business journals, spoken to thousands at events and is part of a future bestselling book on creating more ROI for companies.

Steven is a native Floridian growing up in Melbourne, Florida - finishing his education at the University of Central Florida. Steven spends his time being a husband to wife Alicia and the proud father of two amazing children, Zachary and Sydney.

CHAPTER 29
MAGIC IN THE MAILBOX

by Aaron S. Halderman,
President, Key Touch Media, Inc.

Master salesman Zig Ziglar is famous for saying that "you can have everything in life you want, if you will just help other people get what they want."

A n equally profound statement is:
"If you help enough other people get what they want, you get what you need."

Perhaps The Rolling Stones are at least partly responsible for my interpretation of Mr. Ziglar's well-known words. This always makes sense to entrepreneurs but it definitely isn't common sense. It's a competitive market place but there is always room at the top for a company that has great customer service. Give your customers what they want, and they'll give you what you need.

What they want is a personal connection. They want to know you're not just taking them for granted – that their business means something to you.

I spent some time with Tony Hsieh, CEO of Zappos recently, and took a tour of his company. And Tony will be the first to tell you – he may be known for selling shoes online, but Zappos is really in the business of customer service.

It's how he turns a one-time visitor into a lifetime customer.

And it's why it's so important to implement your own, personal "keep in touch" system and strategy, to keep you connected to your clients.

Before I go on, I should probably introduce myself. My name is Aaron Halderman and I've had the privilege of sharing a stage with some of the real heavy-hitters in the business, including Bob Proctor, Jay Conrad Levinson, Mark Victor Hansen, Michael Gerber, Rich Schefren, and Dan Kennedy. I'm a sales and marketing consultant and part of the Inc. 500 Infusionsoft team, as well as a trainer, a business coach, a speaker and an author. I'm also an avid student of marketing and personal development, as well as the art of launching information-based products and services.

Over the years, I've been able to hone my skills to become a leader in marketing and sales for business owners and business leaders. People look to me for those strategies and programs to implement them.

However, I primarily see myself as a 'rainmaker'.

My main focus is on small businesses, sales teams and entrepreneurs – I'm constantly researching and working with the latest tools and techniques and strategies to help small businesses grow. As you might expect, I deal with a lot of technology, since new systems and software developments tend to come fast and furious in the marketing world.

But the marketing tool I want to focus on now isn't particularly 'cutting edge', at least not from a technological standpoint. It's been around long before the computer was invented. Yet it's still one of the most effective marketing tools in your arsenal.

It's the mail!

Yes, the regular mail …as in snail mail.

I realize that, coming from a 'cutting edge' guy like me, this might be a surprise. Traditional mail has almost been abandoned in favor of the internet – everything from paying a bill to sending a birthday card can be done quickly and efficiently online.

But that's exactly the key to mail's appeal.

When was the last time you opened up the mailbox and found something other than a bill or an advertising mailer – like a card or a note personally addressed to you?

With the exception of a birthday or Christmas, I'm guessing it's probably been a long time.

That's what makes traditional mail so powerful. In these days of cyber greetings and email blasts, getting a real, actual card in the mail that you can open and read and keep on your desk is memorable. It's even special.

That's the magic of the mail. It still has the power to surprise, which can do amazing things for your business.

THE WORLD'S GREATEST SALESMAN

Just ask Joe Girard. He's actually officially listed as the World's Greatest Retail Salesperson in the "Guinness Book of World Records." And he did it all with mail.

Girard was a car salesman – and the undisputed master of the field. Within three years of launching his career, he was selling more new cars and trucks than any other sales person in the world. And he retained that position at the peak of his profession until he retired. In total, in just 15 years, Girard sold exactly 13,001 retail cars. This adds up to more cars per day alone than most dealers sell in an entire year - a pretty amazing story.

But what was even more amazing to me was how he did it. His secret sauce – the thing that set him apart from all of his competitors – was that he stayed in touch with every single person he met, from clients and potential customers, to people he met at meetings and seminars, with cards.

After every meeting or phone call or other form of contact, he would take down that person's details on their business card, or on a file card. He'd include whatever relevant information he could get out of them, from their birthday to their kids' names to their hobbies.

Then, every single month, without fail, he would send every single one of those people a personal card. Not just for Christmas and birthdays, but for anniversaries, Groundhog Day, the Fourth of July, Halloween.

These weren't sales letters. These were just friendly reminders designed to let people know that Joe was thinking about them. That he cared about them as people, not just as customers.

Of course, Joe's greeting card enterprise took a lot of work. This was before the days of computerized databases. Everything was on paper. Yet he still managed to send out over 13,000 handwritten greeting cards every month – with the help of two assistants hired just to help him stay in contact with his client list.

A lot of work? Definitely. But all you need to do is open the Guinness Book of World records to see how it paid off.

THE POWER OF MAIL

Of course, I'm a little biased in this area – I was one of those kids who used to hang around in the driveway, just waiting for the mailman to arrive. Mostly because I hoped there was something in there for me.

Remember those offers that used to be on cereal boxes? You know, send in three UPC tags plus $2.95 and we'll send you a magic kit – or a plastic watch – or a pair of X-ray glasses? I was that kid who sent in for all of that stuff. It was really my first taste of direct response marketing and direct mail, and I couldn't get enough of it.

Even though the actual products were sometimes a letdown – like when those X-ray specs couldn't really help me see through walls (or other more tempting things!), I was hooked.

So it would make sense I would latch on to a way to build the ROI of your business and create lasting personal connections that involved...what else, the mail.

Five years ago, I joined Infusionsoft, the leading CRM software company for small businesses and entrepreneurs, to help bring together their business development channel. It's been an amazing opportunity – allowing me to work with some of the top business coaches and gurus.

Most importantly, it introduced me to what I've found to be one of the most innovative, effective keep-in-touch programs, which brings me back to you, and your business.

You can do the same thing that Joe Girard did to become a master salesman – right now – with a lot less effort than ever before.

As a matter of fact, you can send out a handwritten card, that gets put in the mail, with a real stamp – and you can even send a gift along with that card – with just one click of the mouse, no matter where in the world you are. And for a lot less money than you would spend going to the store yourself and buying a Hallmark card, going to get a stamp, writing a message and mailing it yourself. At UltimateReferralCards.com, you can do it for about a dollar – and we'll even let you try out your first card for free.

It's the easiest way to really cement the personal connection with clients, customers and business associates the Joe Girard way – without having to have two assistants to help you do it.

When people are online, they're busy dealing with business or personal matters. They're also getting continually assaulted with digital information – an e-card is just another inconvenience and often doesn't even get opened.

In contrast, when you go to your mailbox and get an unexpected personal card or gift instead of just the usual bills and supermarket circulars, it's a nice surprise. And isn't it better to be a nice surprise instead of an inconvenience to your customers?

The greeting card industry is a 7.5 billion dollar a year business – because greeting cards are more effective than ever in this increasingly automated world. They still have the power to make a positive impression.

And, even though you can use the cards to help strengthen business bonds, they don't have to be just about business. As a matter of fact, they're more powerful if they're not. You can send out cards that motivate, uplift, inspire… or that just remember a birthday or other special occasion. By adding to a person's daily life, you leave a lasting good impression of yourself and hopefully contribute something positive to that person's well-being.

The cards can include pictures of you, your business, your family, whatever you want to share. And we print them, stuff the envelope, put on the stamp and send it for you at a very low cost. Plus, we can include a gift or a gift card of your choice.

How successful can this kind of card campaign be? Well, one client sent out 81 cards – and 38 of them became customers as a result.

Now, more than ever before, the personal touch means a lot. Our system allows you to implement this strategy quickly and cost efficiently, but with just as powerful an impact. You don't have to send out 13,000 a month like Joe Girard did to be a success…but then again, you might have a better shot at making the Guinness Book of World Records like Joe did!

Please take advantage of this amazing service now by visiting: UltimateReferralCards.com and send a few cards for free on me.

ABOUT AARON

Aaron Halderman is a true Rain Maker. Whether it is working with Inc. 500 Infusionsoft or as a consultant Mr. Halderman knows the sales activities and has attributes needed to bring major opportunities, accounts and profitable relationships to an organization. He has shared the stage with Bob Proctor, Mark Victor Hansen, Michael Gerber and Jay Conrad Levinson to name a few. Aaron will show you how to maximize exposure and influence with books, information products and Rain Maker sales activities. Lots of people may be able to talk the talk, but few actually walk the walk as well. Aaron does both of them impressively. Few business leaders are more on the cutting edge of rainmaking than Aaron.

Aaron graduated *summa cum laude* from Arizona State University and is a member of the National Speakers Association. He currently resides in Phoenix, Arizona with his wife and two daughters.

CHAPTER 30
RECALIBRATE WHAT IS POSSIBLE

by Rem Jackson, Founder & CEO, Top Practices, LLC

I'm grateful that Richard (ROI Guy) invited me to participate in this book to discuss how vital the proper mindset is to you and the success of your business.

Through my company, Top Practices, I consult with doctors, lawyers and other small businesses to help them market themselves and grow their client lists. And I can tell you that the all-important first step to making that happen is *changing your mindset*. That starts with opening your mind to look at things differently.

One of the big goals we have for our clients is to have them recalibrate what they think is possible in their lives. Most people have a frame of reference based on what they already know. For example, we still talk about cars and car engines in terms of horsepower. Well, that's from the dawn of the automobile age, when the new vehicles were replacing horses – *over a hundred years ago.* Is horsepower really the measurement we should still be using in 2010? Unfortunately, it is – only because it's the term we've *always* used.

You can't move forward with backward thinking – it's what stifles innovation and prevents breakthrough ideas. It's what also causes us to get stuck in antiquated systems that don't adapt to changing times – causing an increasing lack of efficiency.

It's not about what you've done. It's about what you can do. It's not about how you've done things. It's about how you can do them better. And it's definitely not about what you think can't be done. It's about how you will be able to achieve more than you ever have before.

ASSUMPTIONS AREN'T REALITY

It's not like I'm immune from this flaw – nobody is, really, which is why we all need to work at overcoming it. We need to associate with people who can help us do so. You cannot simply break out of your old habits by yourself. You need to be continually and constantly reinforced by other winners. Otherwise, you can't see what is truly possible for yourself.

Then again, sometimes you can be taught this lesson by some very unlikely candidates.

For example, when I was a college student at Penn State University, I worked in a brickyard one summer for a man named Reggie, who was a lot shorter and a lot older than I was.

My job in this brickyard was to fill hundred-pound tanks of mortar – not the most glamorous of occupations, but a job is a job. After I filled these tanks, I would seal the tops and get them onto a pallet that was shifted to people who had bricks that needed to be glued together. The filled tanks were really heavy, really bulky and I could never pick them up by myself.

One afternoon, one of the tanks I had just filled up was sitting in the exact place where Reggie wanted to drive his forklift. "Beep, beep!" Reggie laid on the forklift's horn.

I looked up and I asked "What?" "Move it," Reggie replied. "No way" I responded. "I can't pick that up. I have to get a hand lift." "Beep beep beep!" honked Reggie, as he yelled, "Pick it up now!"

"I can't," I came back at him, "*You* do it if you want it done now!" Reggie stopped the beeping and got down from the forklift. And he was about as big as the tank was, again, a lot smaller than me. He walked over to the tank, picked it right up without a problem, moved it out of his way, and gave me a look that was a potent combination of disgust and pity. Then he got back on his forklift and went on his merry way.

I stood there as it finally sunk in that I could have done that just as easily – probably a lot more easily – than Reggie had. After all, I was 19 years old, in shape, strong and about two feet taller than the guy. But until someone showed me it was possible to move those heavy tanks, I had it in my mind that there was no way I could do it. So I never even really tried.

After Reggie recalibrated my mind, however, I moved those tanks anytime I wanted to - without thinking twice about it.

I had the same kind of unexpected jolt later in my adult life from someone I thought had absolutely nothing to teach me. But it changed my professional path forever.

I was at a conference where the top marketers in their category for the year were being honored. They had worked very hard for this recognition and most of them really impressed me.

Except for one man.

He spoke well enough, but he was ridiculously over exuberant and someone I would usually never listen to. But he began talking about how he sought out other top performers who told him what things worked for them. How he became convinced that, since they worked for those people, they would work for him. So he just applied all their winning techniques to his business, without doubting they would work or second-guessing himself.

And he changed his life – instead of being out on the road 50 weeks out of the year making about a million dollars, he was able to work from home *and* triple his income.

Suddenly, someone that I would have done everything in my power to avoid was a giant inspiration. I knew I had to rethink what success was – and, just as Reggie had showed me that I could lift a tank filled with mortar, this person demonstrated that I could completely transform my goals and achieve more than I thought was possible. I ended up quadrupling what I did before because of this unexpected empowerment.

What's your reaction to this story? Is it, "Well, that guy can do that, but that's him. I can't." If it is, you might as well stop reading this now. If you're ready to recalibrate, however, I'm about to share a few secrets on how you can make this process work for you.

There are three important steps you can take that can help you recalibrate your goals – and your life. They work for me, they work for my clients and they're bound to make things happen for you.

STEP ONE – CREATE SMART GOALS

Before you put into effect any major changes in your life, it's crucial that you write down your overall goals – and that you make sure those goals are S.M.A.R.T.

- **Specific.** If you're too general with a goal, it will be much harder to accomplish. In other words, just saying, "I want to be rich," doesn't tell you HOW you're going to get rich. You need to identify what you want to accomplish, who is involved, where it needs to happen and when. Most importantly, you need to answer the question of *why* do you want to reach this particular objective.
- **Measurable** – You have to have some concrete way of measuring your progress as you work towards each goal you set.
- **Attainable** – Is this a goal you can reach? Do you have the necessary skills and resources? If you don't, where can you access them?
- **Realistic** - To be realistic, your goal must be one that you're sure you're both *willing* and *able* to work towards.
- **Time Bound**- If you don't put deadlines on a goal, you won't have the motivation to reach it. A set timeline for working towards a goal creates the urgency you need to complete the task at hand.

The most successful goal writers produce 3 to 5 goals in the following categories:

- Personal
- Business
- Financial
- Health
- Fun

And they produce those 3 to 5 goals for each of the above categories in the following time frames:

- Lifetime
- 3 Year
- 1 Year
- Quarterly

As one of our most famous American motivational writers, Napoleon Hill, put it, you should know your "Definiteness of Purpose" – your overriding desire for your life and work – and focus on what will get you there. It allows you to spend your resources in the most appropriate way, knowing that, if it's not going to advance your goals, you shouldn't do it.

STEP TWO – USE THE POWER OF ASSOCIATION

As I mentioned earlier, an important aspect to recalibrating what's possible is surrounding yourself with other people who are proven "winners" – those that have a track record of achievement who continue to work towards higher goals for themselves.

Motivational speaker Jim Rohn says that we are all the average of the five people we hang out with the most – and I believe that. Look around at who you associate with most frequently – are they helping you, or bringing you down?

The Power of Association is why you should get into a Mastermind Group as soon as possible. Nothing has been more useful to me than my Mastermind Groups. Having a key Mastermind alliance – a small group of people you're completely in tune with – motivates and inspires you. If it's a successful group, then you would do anything for each other in support of a common goal.

Andrew Carnegie, the founder of U.S. Steel and one of America's most successful businesspeople, decided to create his steel mill because he was in a Mastermind alliance with key people that helped him create a business dynasty.

Having said that, your Mastermind Groups shouldn't just be about business – in our Top Practices Mastermind Groups, we don't just focus on increasing revenues, we also tackle the problem of balancing our lives so we have some time to enjoy what we earn with the ones we love.

Your Mastermind Groups also shouldn't just be limited to business associates that are at your level. You should also consider Masterminding with:

(a). Your employees. A big percentage of your business dreams are in the hands of the people doing the actual work. You should only hire people you consider to be "superstars" at what they do – or those with the potential to become superstars. Again, who you surround yourself with can often determine if you're able to achieve your goals.

(b). Your spouse. If you aren't in alignment with the person you're married to, you can't possibly have a happy and productive home. Find ways to support and empower each other.

(c). Education. Find ways to grow your knowledge by accessing "the good stuff." Avoid endless cable news shows where people are inevitably arguing about trivia for hours at a time. Ignore the garbage that most people fill their minds with and look for books and programs that will add to your consciousness, not distract it.

(d). Yourself. Cultivate the garden of your mind so there aren't any weeds in it. Eliminate negative thinking that stops you in your tracks. When you feel weak or helpless, remember a day when a stronger version of yourself prevailed and try to access that strength when you need it.

STEP THREE – CREATE YOUR ACTION PLANS

Remember the marketer I wrote about earlier? The one who inspired me to recalibrate my possibilities? Well, if all he had done was create goals without following through on them, he obviously wouldn't have been much inspiration to me. But he didn't sit around thinking forever about what to do to get what he wanted – he went out and took *massive* action, and made things work for him.

That's what Step Three is all about – creating action plans, based on your goals and your Masterminding, and following through on those plans. The words "following through" are the most important. If you don't act, nothing happens.

And, when it comes to my clients, I make sure marketing is an integral part of those action plans. Everyone's products are usually roughly the same quality – it's the marketing that really makes the difference. Unless you can sell your product or service beyond your customer base, you're not going to grow much bigger, if at all.

A great way to approach this is to create a marketing organizational board that clearly lays out, in a 'dashboard' fashion, everything you plan to do that promotes your business daily, weekly, every season and every year.

Your marketing system should have five components to it:

1. An attraction system to generate leads (what really works well is the current Dan Kennedy-inspired trend of information marketing – offering free educational materials about what you do in order to build a contact list)

2. Growing your list of leads as big as you can
3. Systems to convert these leads into new customers and clients
4. Building referrals from existing clients (offering discounts to your customers to encourage this is always a good idea).
5. Reappoint and Reactivate. Follow up with clients that have drifted away and also find new products and services to offer existing customers. People already doing business with you are the easiest to sell to.

These five components should be automated as much as possible. A quote I love comes from Alfred North Whitehead – "Civilization advances by extending the number of operations we can perform without thinking about them."

The more you can implement automated database systems that you can "set and forget," such as the ones Richard (ROI Guy) offers, the better off you and your business will be. You'll get more marketing done more consistently and you won't have to neglect your core business.

Most people who come to my company contact us because they know their marketing isn't working. They know they're not getting the right results, and, most importantly, they know there's a better way.

Once we teach them how to do it right, they still stay connected to us - because we have created a group of positive, forward-thinking people that have recalibrated what they thought was possible, and moved forward together to greater and higher levels of success. That's the definition of an effective Mastermind group.

A strong mindset makes the difference. You and the other readers of this book are going to read a lot of innovative and interesting ideas from its contributors. Implementing those ideas, however, without having clear goals or knowing why or where you want to go, can easily lead to failure.

I urge you to write down your goals and review them regularly. Follow the mindset process I've outlined in this chapter. And you'll have the greatest chance at success.

Good luck with all you want to accomplish.

214

ABOUT REM

Rem Jackson is the President and CEO of Top Practices, LLC, and the leader of the Top Practices Master Mind Group. Top Practices is a company dedicated to helping professionals and businesses reach their professional and personal goals by building their "perfect practice or business".

Rem has been guiding professionals, educators, and business leaders as a coach and trainer for over 18 years. He led the team that founded Classroom Connect, a high-tech company dedicated to helping K-12 educators integrate technology into their instruction. He contributed to the sale of Classroom Connect to Reed-Elsevier in 2001, and continued to serve as Vice President of Professional Development. At Classroom Connect, he led the development of seminars, conferences, custom professional development programs, and Web-based training. The programs he developed have been experienced by over 120,000 educators, businesspeople, and government leaders in North America and Asia.

Rem's extensive experience in sales, marketing, and senior management in the areas of education, health care, and industry uniquely qualify him to lead the development and implementation of Top Practices proprietary products and services.

Rem has keynoted over 45 state and national conferences and appeared on television in Singapore, New Zealand, and on the San Francisco Bay Area program "Silicon Spin," discussing technology and its appropriate uses in instruction and professional development. His ability to guide participants through challenging content in an interesting and informative style has contributed to his national reputation as an entertaining, informative, and dynamic speaker.

Rem Jackson is available for a limited number of speaking engagements. He can be reached at info@TopPractices.com. You can find out more about Top Practices at www.TopPractices.com

CHAPTER 31
THE ULTIMATE BUSINESS EVENT: CREATING EVENTS THAT ARE PROFITABLE!

by Eddie Diaz – Creative Producer, Event Planner and CEO, Encore Creations

F irst of all, I want to thank Richard for letting me be a part of this book. Because really, what I do is all about ROI. But not in the way you might think.

I'm an event planner and creative producer – and like most event planners, I book venues, hire entertainment and oversee the food, the décor and pretty much every aspect of a dinner, or a party, or a presentation. From small events to the large scale spectacles, I handle everything worry-free – removing the pain and the mistakes most businesses make when putting on an event.

But as I see it, making sure those details are under control are only part of my job.

Most event planners are all about – and only about – the event itself. If it looks good, if people have fun, if it goes off without a hitch, they consider what they've done a success. Traditionally, ROI is not even a consideration, let alone a strategic event component.

But I approach event planning a little differently. At my company, we're producers of show business *for business*. Which means that every event we put on, from a small dinner to a large scale show, has to have a *purpose*. Your event experience is all about your brand, your goals and your returns! From the planning and invitations, to the event itself, right through to the follow-up after the event – everything is designed and produced to showcase your business. My strategic goal is to fulfill your objectives.

In my view, events are all about creating an experience that delivers results, period! Unfortunately for many, improper planning, no marketing expertise, lack of creativity and limited valuable resources ends in a less than effective event. A total waste of money! Producing a successful event is more than just organizing event resources; it is about masterfully choreographed creative and strategic solutions catered to specific goals.

That's why for me, putting on a successful event isn't just about being creative *or* just about being strategic. It's about creating an experience specifically designed to guarantee to deliver the return on the investment. Events are more than fluff, they're serious money-making experiences!

Which is why, in my field, I'm the Producer of Show Business for Business! I create events that are profit driven, brand engaging and relationship building – guaranteed!

IT ALL STARTED...

Back in Puerto Rico, where I grew up, I wasn't the ROI event producer. I was the Lemon Boy.

It was actually my dad's idea – we had a lemon tree in our backyard, and he basically said, "Here are some lemons, here are some bags. Put them together, and you can make some money." Which, to my 7 or 8-year old self, was a pretty exciting prospect. I set up a stand on the street corner and started my first business, selling bags of lemons to the neighbors.

That was, I guess you'd say, my start-up.

From there, an entrepreneur was born. I held car washes. I sold candy from a little cart I used to push around. But I also really, really loved to entertain people. So I figured out how to combine both of my passions, putting on shows in my backyard and charging the neighborhood kids 25 cents each to get in. I handled every aspect of the production right down to the concessions, so that candy cart definitely came in handy. For me, it was all about the experience!

At 17, I decided it was time to put all I had learned about the business of entertainment to the test. So I relocated to the USA with a dream of working for Disney. After all, they are the masters when it comes to putting together a total entertainment experience – so what better place to perfect my craft? I absorbed all I could there, and went on to the creative department at Universal and a job handling entertainment for Premiere Cruise Lines.

All signs pointed toward a future in show biz. So I happily accepted a theater scholarship to the University of Central Florida.

But that budding entrepreneur inside me wasn't quite satisfied. I combined business and entertainment as a kid. Wasn't there a way I could do the same thing as an adult – and make a living at it?

THE LAUNCH...

I decided to change course and left UCF to get a business degree from the University of Phoenix. Then, armed with my creative expertise and my business knowledge, I was ready to launch my own company supplying entertainment and events to businesses.

I expected my venture to be a huge success. But it wasn't – at least not right away.

When I shared what I did for a living with business owners, they saw it, they understood it, but they didn't quite buy it. Because I couldn't provide an answer to the eternal question, "What's In It for Me?"

And honestly, what *was* in it for them? They would give me their money, but what would they get in return? A great party, an entertaining show, but so what? How was that going to boost their bottom line? They needed a good reason and a profound answer as to why would they trust me with their hard-earned money.

I was meeting with some Orlando business leaders and mastermind mentors when I had my "Aha!" moment.

I knew that if I was going to get anywhere, I had to show them how MY business could help THEIR business. What was I really providing? Yes, there was the food, and the décor, and the entertainment – and the peace of mind that comes from knowing it's all taken care of.

But what I was really providing was a showcase for their business. So I needed to change the way I explained the service I provided.

Instead of talking about the great food and the awesome entertainment and the pretty decorations, I put it this way:

"I provide a full, emerging experience designed and built around your specific objectives and the return that you're looking for.

In other words, I create show business for business.

And it's all about the ROI."

I knew in my heart that there could be – HAD to be – more to an event experience than your basic event components. My passion led me to discover ways to help business growth, strengthen client relationships, expand brand awareness and deliver measurable results. That is the true purpose of an event.

A PARTY WITH A PURPOSE

Anyone can ask their secretary to order some rubber chicken, book a room and throw a party, or a dinner, or a show. But to create an event that provides ROI – you need a specialist, an expert.

But a lot of people don't know this. So they have their event, and then they complain: "I spent all this money and I didn't get anything out of it."

I say: "That's because you didn't have emotional triggers built into your event."

They just didn't have a strategy.

A lot of businesses are like this. They come to me and say: "I just want to get people in here." Well, that doesn't help me, and it definitely doesn't help you. As a business, you should always know where you're going!

To showcase your business, I need the same thing. I need specifics. I need clarity. I need the topics, the goals, the objectives of just what the event is supposed to accomplish. Once I know your goal – whether it's to welcome new clients, or celebrate a success, or prospect for new business – I can begin the process of strategically creating the perfect experience to achieve that goal.

Of course, part of that strategy is making sure everything looks good. If people are going to bother to show up, one goal is always for them to be impressed. So we pull out all the stops to create a totally unique experience that showcases your company in a new way. We put on an amazing show, and we make you the star.

It's all about people and emotions. What do you want to convey to your guests? How do you want them to feel? Everything is designed specifically to get your employees, or your customers, or your prospects, or whoever your guests are - to sense, feel, think, act and relate to your brand the way you want them to. And, of course, have an amazing time while doing it.

For me, that starts with the five senses. I want your guests to see, feel, smell, touch and even taste your brand. By communicating your message across the board, in as many different ways as possible, we reinforce your message to your guests on every level. This builds the relationship between your guests and your brand – we share the culture of your business and make your guests a part of that culture, which helps them form that emotional connection. It helps them *love* you.

THE STRUCTURE

For me, an event breaks down into three segments. There's a pre-event, the event itself and a post event. And all of them are equally important.

The pre-event is basically the "invitation period," when you get people to come. This is an area where many non-experts tend to fall short. Either they wait until the last minute, or they only send a single invitation. The result? A low turnout – and lost money and opportunity.

For us, the pre-event period is about doing everything we can to get people excited to show up for your party. I look at it like a political campaign! My strategy is to hit people multiple times – with a "save the date," a formal invitation, emails and even a personal phone call – to make sure you have the audience you need for your event. We make doubly, triply, even *quadruply* sure, that your audience shows up, primed and excited for the experience we're going to create for them – and for you.

Of course, the big deal is the event itself – and we do make it a big deal. The entire event is completely choreographed from the moment your guest pulls up and enters the space. We leave absolutely nothing to chance! Everything is designed to get them to see, feel, touch, think and act your brand. This is something I learned from my days at Disney. If you've ever waited in line for a ride there, you probably remember that EVERYTHING is about that ride until you are out the door and back in the park. It's all about storytelling – you build up to a crescendo, and then you taper down. There's a beginning, a middle and an end. I choreograph my events the same way, with those little emotional touches all night long; keeping your guests engaged every step of the way.

But while the event is the big deal, in my opinion (and it's an expert opinion!), the post-event period is the most important. After all, this is where the "R" part of the ROI actually happens. This is where you find out if you made that connection – if you had that impact.

And this is also, unfortunately, the area where most novice planners blow it – **<u>because they forget to follow up!</u>**

Follow-up after an event reminds people of the great time they had and encourages them to reconnect with your company again. It gets them while they're thinking and feeling good about your company. So we take it seriously.

We start our post-event period at the event itself. I like to collect testimonials, taking photos or video. And I make sure every guest leaves with a take-home item that will keep you and your company and your party on their mind, in the days after the event.

Then a week after the event, we follow up (or you follow up according to a plan we devise for you). We send out an email or thank you card with a great photo taken at the party included. We place follow-up calls. We send reminders to collect giveaways.

It's all about reinforcing the great experience your guests had with your company, and your brand. They'll feel a new bond and connection with you and your company. They'll feel like a part of your family. And they'll no doubt be waiting for their next invitation.

SO! CREATE YOUR VERY OWN
EVENT EXPERIENCE TODAY!

If you want to know what we can do for you, I invite you to sign on for my **Ultimate Business Gift** – a complimentary gift valued at $995.00. Your gift comes with a **Strategic Business Event Analysis**, **$500.00 Event Dollars**, a FREE copy of my **Building Business with Events CD** and a subscription to our monthly **Backstage Report.** It's a really powerful tool for getting huge ROI out of your next event, whether it's a sit-down dinner for 10 next month or a casino night for 200 next June. By looking at your business and discussing your goals, I can custom create an event for you. Claim your Free Gift by visiting my website: www.encorecreations.com

ABOUT EDDIE

Eddie Diaz is the creative conjuror, driving force and owner of Encore Creations, a strategic special event company that specializes in the creation, design and production of shows and events for business and social occasions. An award winning producer, designer and director, Eddie began his entrepreneurial journey as a child producing and directing his own backyard musical reviews and selling lemons at a stand. He has studies in graphic design, television production, interior design, theater and business at the University of the Sacred Heart, University of Central Florida, and earned a B.S in Business from the University of Phoenix.

Eddie has 20 years of experience in the entertainment industry. From small businesses to INC 500 companies, his credits include creation, design and production of stage shows, themed environments, and special events for **Walt Disney Entertainment, Universal Studios Entertainment, Premier Cruise Lines, Minor League Baseball, General Electric, Scholastic Book Fairs, Pirates Dinner Adventures**, to name a few. His creativity and energy has been recognized by industry professionals like **Florida Biz Bash, Event-Solutions Magazine, Orlando Style Magazine and Catersource.** Winner of the Event Solutions Spotlight Award 2006 Rising Star, 2009 Creative Director of the Year and nominated for 2010 Event Producer of the Year.

CHAPTER 32
THE HOLY GRAIL OF ACHIEVING ROI

by W. Roger Salam, Chairman and Founder, The Winner's Circle International, Inc.

"None of us is as smart as all of us."
~ Japanese Proverb

W hat if there was ONE THING you could do to assure your success? ONE THING that would clear all the obstacles in your way and create a true path to financial freedom, or get the most for your ROI efforts?

Well, there is. And it's not an idea I just came up with on my own. Rather, it's a proven foundational principle of how to grow rich, according to the father of the modern day personal development movement, Napoleon Hill.

That principle is Masterminding. When it comes to getting an everlasting ROI, investing your time in a Mastermind group will pay off in ways you never dreamt of.

They say you are as successful as the five people you associate with the most. Masterminding is all about associating and brainstorming with *only* successful people – successful people who have already gone through your struggles, who know the short cuts and the secrets to overcoming the odds and finding your fortune.

THE HISTORY OF MASTERMINDING

One of America's most successful business tycoons, Andrew Carnegie, never got an MBA to learn how to run a business. No, he learned it from his own unofficial Mastermind group. At the age of 14, he got a job as a messenger boy for a telegraph company – and saw all the messages from the local business barons. He found himself in a position to learn everyone's financial dealings, partnerships and business plans – and by the age of 17, he had a complete business education, learning from those who were local successes.

Throughout his rise to the top, he continued to surround himself with those who knew more than he did. As part of the first official American business Mastermind group, the Chicago 6, he swapped secrets with the founder of Wrigley's Chewing Gum, the owner of the Yellow Cab Company, the head of the world's largest ad agency, and other business titans. He also put the Mastermind principle in action with his own business management team.

In 1908, Carnegie commissioned Napoleon Hill to study the most successful people of their era and find out what qualities they possessed, or methodology they employed, to become the leading businesspeople of their time. Out of that study came Hill's ground-breaking book, "Think Rich, Grow Rich," which contained the 17 principles for supreme success. Carnegie was probably not surprised to see one of the three main foundation principles was Masterminding.

And the surprising fact is that Carnegie was far from the first to come up with the idea. Masterminding, as a matter of fact, was employed by one of America's founding fathers – Benjamin Franklin, who created what he termed a "club of mutual improvement" with local entrepreneurs. If you had any doubt that Masterminding brings forth big ideas, out of Franklin's group came the first library, paved streets, night watchmen and public hospitals.

The truth is Carnegie and Hill formalized a process that almost every successful person has employed throughout history – brainstorming with other great minds so that everyone can benefit from the combined talents and knowledge contained in the group.

Hill writes: "No two minds ever come together without thereby creating a third, invisible intangible force, which may be likened to a third mind. When a group of individual minds are coordinated and function in harmony, the increased energy created through that alliance becomes available to every individual in the group.

"No man can become a permanent success without taking others along with him."

And that is precisely why our new Mastermind alliance, The Winner's Circle, has become such an important resource to so many successful people. The Winners Circle, has been specifically designed to help entrepreneurs build their business to the next level, through powerful and creative interactions with other high-powered successful professionals who can provide the answers to virtually any business challenge. It's a private, invitation-only circle that isn't about just getting a few good ideas – it's about obtaining the tools to "turbo-charge" your business and eliminating the limitations you may have unconsciously placed on just how successful your business can be.

We've taken the 20th century concept of Masterminding into the 21st century – call it Mastermind 2.0 – in order to give this already-powerful process more modern-day muscle.

PUTTING TOGETHER THE WINNER'S CIRCLE

As for myself, I became well acquainted with the power of personal development in my early career, when I worked my way up to become the number one trainer and speaker for Tony Robbins. I left Robbins in the late 90's to get in on the then-hot internet business boom – and became part of a company that went from nothing to 2 billion dollars in capitalization when we went public. I thought I was set for life – I was running three divisions of the company and was just waiting for the stock to hit 100, at which point I would diversify. But then the 'tech bubble burst', and in one day my fortune went from dot com to dot gone.

I lost everything – which didn't bother me. I knew most great business leaders suffered great reversals in their lives which they later overcame, and I felt confident I could do the same. And one night, when I was watching late night TV, I saw my next opportunity – an infomercial with a real estate guru who said you could make millions buying homes even if you had no money and no credit. And I thought to myself, "No money? No credit? I qualify!!!"

I jumped in with both feet and bought my first home for $16,000. From there, I rode the real estate train to riches – which enabled me to acquire my biggest estate yet, a 38,000 square foot mansion. Yes, you read that right – 38,000 square feet. It's the largest home in the public record in my county – and probably several other surrounding counties as well.

Now I didn't buy this huge estate so I could live in it, believe it or not. I try to lead a simple life and I don't want my ego to get in the way of that. No, I bought the property in order to use it strictly as a "Mastermind Mansion" for our Winner's Circle members. It definitely has enough room and, when we get tired of Masterminding, we can always play basketball on the court that's located on the second floor!

I don't tell you all this to impress you – but to impress upon you the possibilities that Masterminding brings to those who participate in it. We work hard to surround our members with the aura of success. They're met by a private limo at the airport and brought to the mansion, where a private chef cooks for them. We liberate our guests from their personal needs – so they can concentrate and get the most out of the total Mastermind experience

If you gather together with other successful people in an amazing setting like this mansion, it inspires you and empowers you to find ways to achieve more. I lost everything – and yet, I am fortunate enough to be able to offer this "Mastermind Mansion" to my Winner's Circle members for meeting and relaxing.

Everything I've gotten in life I attribute to Masterminding with like-minded successful people. To me it's the powerful final step of getting what you want – and I want to talk a little more about how we accomplish that inside The Winner's Circle.

INSIDE THE WINNER'S CIRCLE

First of all, as I mentioned, membership in The Winner's Circle is private and by invitation only. You may feel free to inquire at our website to see if you qualify, and we'll be happy to consider you, but we need to keep our Mastermind members at a level where everyone has something of value to offer each other. We charge $10,000 to join The Winner's Circle to help ensure that everyone is already at a certain level of success.

My personal philosophy is that I don't care what you want out of life – whether you want to be the ideal parent, save the whales, head up an international empire or run the most successful running shoe store in east New Jersey. Whatever you want happens faster, better, cheaper and stronger through Masterminding.

You learn from other's mistakes, which saves you time, money and helps you solve countless other problems. People who have gone before you share their experiences and you learn from their direct knowledge.

Here are the 7 Power Points of what the advantages our Winner's Circle members – and any authentic Mastermind group - enjoy:

1. **Accelerated Results** – By learning what mistakes to avoid and which shortcuts pay off from experienced successful people, you speed up the trial-and-error process most entrepreneurs suffer through over and over again.
2. **Synergy and Cooperation** – Cooperation, frankly, beats competition. When you work with others, you create a positive energy that's more than the sum of its parts. *The Winner's Circle is where 1 + 1 equals 11, not 2.*
3. **Specific Solutions to Challenges** – Rather than just hear bland advice like "Never Give Up" and "Hang in There," you've got experienced

business people who have likely been in the kind of difficult situations you're dealing with. They know how they got through it – and they can give you effective, meaningful action plans so you can too.

4. **Increased Profitability** – Our Mastermind members are bottom-line oriented; otherwise they wouldn't be the successful people they are. They know the secrets to 'cutting the fat' and boosting sales, and they share them.

5. **Camaraderie and Valuable Lifelong Friends** – Mastermind members inevitably bond as they share their own personal stories and strategies. You gain your own personal "board of directors" for your life and business – of which you're the chairman!

6. **Cutting Edge Resources** – By gaining access to other business successes, you have access to the leading resources they use to build their companies and their brands. This allows you to keep in touch with the latest trends and the newest profit-making tools available.

7. **Joint Ventures** - One of the most exciting things to see is when two or more Mastermind members create a new business together during a meeting. Expertise and experience often overlap in a way that sparks new ideas and new partnerships in success.

The fundamental idea behind The Winner's Circle is that "Success breeds success." Whoever you listen to will determine your destiny. Inside The Winner's Circle, there are *only* people worth listening to.

King Arthur and his Knights of the Round Table is the perfect metaphor for what a Mastermind group is all about. It's the essence of what I have built The Winner's Circle to become.

Masterminding is all about seeing what is possible. Someone once asked Helen Keller what was worse than not having sight. She wisely replied, "Having sight and no vision." Vision is all about possibilities and seeing what something can be, not what it is at the moment.

I wish you luck if you plan to build your own Mastermind group to empower your success. If you do wish to jumpstart the process and apply for membership in The Winner's Circle, visit: www.joinmywinnerscircle.com to see if you qualify.

If you want to achieve true and lasting success, you need to be with the kind of people who can elevate your status, who can infuse you with the passion to go after what you want and hold you to a higher standard. That is what the optimum Mastermind group is all about.

Here's to your success – and the Mastermind group that will help you achieve it!

ABOUT ROGER

Roger is The Chairman & founder of The Winner's Circle, the Largest Mastermind Forum for top Speakers, Successful Entrepreneurs, and Information & Internet Marketers.

Roger is also the founder of Real Estate Web Academy www.RealEstateWebAcademy.com, an educational and social networking community of tens of thousands of Real Estate investors.

Roger is currently the resident contributor and Financial Freedom mentor for "Yes, You Can Do It Club" a worldwide membership club for entrepreneurs with members from all seven continents that is growing through internet social networking (www.YesYouCanDoItClub.com).

Prior to getting involved in Real Estate investing, Roger served as a professional speaker and trainer with the world renowned motivational speaker and peak performance coach Anthony Robbins. He has delivered over 3700 professional talks to various corporations, non-profit organizations and educational institutions in North America, Europe and Asia.

Roger Salam is co-author of two books on Marketing and "Secrets of the Real Estate Millionaires" and his latest book; "Mastermind Your Way to Millions" is due out end of the second quarter of 2010. He's a graduate of UCLA, married to his high school sweetheart and has three lovely daughters. He is most passionate about sharing knowledge and resources and empowering people to reach financial freedom and higher levels of performance & success through the power of Mastermind!

CHAPTER 33
TRADE SHOWS: GO BEYOND THE BOOTH

by Rajiv Kapur, Configurations

W e've become a successful trade show marketing company, working with such Blue Chip companies as IBM, AT&T, Northrop Grumman, and the Harris Corporation for one simple reason: *We never give our clients the booth they came to buy. We go beyond!* At least that's what I believe.

Most companies do not have a defined purpose for their trade show program. The majority of the companies I've interviewed exhibit because they feel they need to show mainly because they know the competition is going to be there, so *they* have to be there as well. It's a defensive strategy, a "show up" attitude, rather than a "win" attitude.

At Configurations, we take a completely different view. For us, being in a trade show is a giant communications opportunity, an incredible way to positively interact with your best customers, gain quality leads, and effectively market your brand in a tangible, physical way.

By approaching a trade show exhibit as a part of an overall marketing process, of which the trade show is the mid-point, not the end-point, we provide our clients with an awesome ROI. We segment the process into three major steps: (1) pre-show campaigns; (2) at-show presentations; and (3) post-show follow up campaigns. No lame or gimmicky at-show promotions, like cruise vacations or plasma TVs, to inflate booth traffic. Just great integrated steps that create positive results. As a matter of fact, I strongly discourage non-related giveaways!

So let's go "beyond the booth" and talk about how to make your exhibit an experience.

TACKLING TRADE SHOW TRADITIONS

I began in the business about 25 years ago with a graphics reproduction company. More and more of our work became providing large format graphics to trade show exhibits. We did more and more trade show work and I became more and more fascinated with it. I majored in marketing and saw a number of ways we could improve on what was being done. So we decided to sell off the graphics side and concentrate solely on trade show exhibits and marketing through events.

Frankly, I didn't believe the trade show medium was being properly utilized. Most of our competitors were just about *selling* an exhibit and most exhibitors were just about *buying* an exhibit. They did not understand the benefit and power of trade show marketing and the full reason that attendees come to them. Attendees come to get knowledge, learn about what's new in the market place, cut through the clutter of two-dimensional promotions, and be able to differentiate between providers to select the best fit. The attendees want to experience and learn about the company as a whole, not just the nuts-and-bolts of the product or service.

I was amazed at how companies worked harder and were more concerned about what they were going to give away, rather than on any marketing strategy. It's easy to get a couple of hundred leads if you're giving away a car or some other big-ticket item – especially if you have some hot "booth babes" out front to lure in the guys. But how good are those leads going to be? Where is the ROI?

The bulk of the prospects are basically coming in so they can win the item – and they're not really interested in buying from the company itself. The result is you get an overwhelming amount of junk leads mixed in with the few quality leads. Those leads, unfiltered and unrated, go back to the office, where sales people following up on them quickly get discouraged by the time and energy they're wasting contacting people who just don't want to buy. They stop trying and the quality leads get lost in the shuffle.

Generally, however, an exhibiting company is happy if they get to see 20 or 30 of their main clients face-to-face and strengthen those relationships. That's important and great, but there is such a bigger opportunity to be had – and a much bigger ROI that's easily attainable.

The fact is, yes, if your exhibit is nice, professional and attractive, you will get a certain amount of people automatically stopping by. And that's usually the measure of success to a company. But it definitely is *not* to us – because we are intent on delivering a whole lot more to each and every one of our clients.

Our approach to trade shows is that it is a communications medium – and we want to be able to create an environment that conveys the essence of the brand and its products - in a way that effectively differentiates the company from the competition and firmly embeds its overall message.

Now, let's talk about how we get that done.

OUR FIVE-STEP APPROACH

When we're looking at how to best serve a client who needs an exhibit, we ask them a series of questions:

- Why are you going to the trade show?
- What are you hoping to accomplish?
- What is your message?
- How does the show need to compliment your overall sales and branding strategy?

The answers to those questions give us our direction, and help us determine the message, size, texture, materials, color schemes, and shapes of the physical booth. More importantly, it gives us the foundation for our five-step approach to making their exhibit *more* than an exhibit – to making it an overall successful marketing venture that accomplishes their goals.

OUR FIVE-STEP APPROACH GOES AS FOLLOWS:

1. POSITION

By asking our client the questions I've already listed, we can understand where the company is today and where it wants to be. We also understand how it needs to be positioned for its goals and against its competition. These are things we keep in mind and use as a lens throughout the entire strategic and creative brainstorming process.

2. ATTRACT

We want to attract the *right* kind of customer to the booth. To do this, we begin with what we call our "pre-show program" – marketing in advance to the people we want to come to the exhibit. We do this with everything from special ads, mailers, social media and direct contacts. Generally, you need to use a combination of all of these, depending on the standard of customer. The messaging in the exhibit is 'in sync' with the pre-show campaigns for easy identification by the target audience. The graphics and message on the exhibit are also designed to be eye-catching, relevant, and intriguing to the attendees at the show who might have missed the pre-show campaigns.

We break this pre-show marketing into two categories – (a) the new people we want to capture and (b) the current customers we want to retain and possibly sell more products and services to. We continue this marketing to qualify leads when the trade show is actually in progress to ensure a good flow of people that the company *should* be talking to, not people who just want to win a plasma TV.

3. ENGAGE

How does the company deal with the prospects coming to their booth? How do we make sure they take maximum advantage of the few minutes they have to talk to them? This is where what we call "Boothmanship®" comes into play.

We train the personnel who will be manning the exhibit on how to interact with prospects. Most sales people aren't good at a sales pitch of just a few minutes – they're used to 45-minute "appointments" where they have more than enough time to make small talk and pitch their company.

At a booth, however, there's a different speed and cadence to the presentation needed to effectively engage a visitor. In America, the typical interaction time at an exhibit booth is 3 to 5 minutes (it's generally over twice as long in other countries). We encourage personnel to stretch that to 7 to 12 minutes and create a meaningful conversation that begins with trying to ascertain both the visitor's primary and secondary needs. Then, when you present to the visitor, you focus your interaction to demonstrate how your company can meet those needs, both with the tangible and *intangible* advantages of your product or service.

Everyone sells the "tangible" advantages –the actual benefit of the product or service. This is a "me too" approach in today's competitive world of multiple suppliers. But the "intangible" is just as important, if not more so. Many companies sell the same thing, but the "intangible" features are such things as your unique company culture, brand, customer service, positive testimonials, and success stories. These are what make you unique and put you into a "me only" category. These are the things that can really set you apart from the competition, so they're crucial.

4. COMPREHEND

Learn and educate -this stage is critical for both the exhibitor and for the prospect. Being attentive to the attendee's needs and conversation, and responding accordingly, enriches both parties and creates bonds. By demonstrating these intangibles, the visitor begins to comprehend why they should deal with YOUR company rather than with another. Most people are at differing stages of the buying process and are coming to trade shows to shop and compare. By effectively communicating your company's high standards and brand in an emotionally-bonding manner, you will give your visitors what we call "the warm fuzzies" and make them feel better about dealing with you over your competition.

5. MEMORABLE

As you're probably aware, people don't buy until they're ready. Odds are most new prospects won't be ready to buy at the trade show. That's why you have to make your exhibit and interaction with them *memorable,* so that when they *are* ready to buy, they're not shuffling through all the companies' cards and brochures trying to remember who everyone is…and maybe mixing you up with someone else.

This, again, is why we encourage booth personnel to take more time with each visitor and have a meaningful conversation. This helps build as strong and *memorable* a relationship as possible. The extra time aids their recall, and, if you have a number of different props and places in the booth that allow the visitor more physical interaction with various facets of your company, those interactions will also stay in their mind.

It's also important, on your end, to collect good information on the visitor to relay back to your sales force at the office, so when they call the lead later, they can effectively relate to them. In other words, make it easy to resume the relationship when the time comes.

Depending upon the buying cycle, create a post-show follow-up program to tie in with the pre-show and at-show messaging.

Hopefully, you can understand from this five-step approach how we manage the flow from start to finish. It's important to realize that, at trade shows, the sales process either *begins*, *accelerates,* or *ends*. Whatever stage of that process a visitor is in at the time - just beginning to scope out their options or narrowing them down to a final pick - you want to be able to fully engage them and make as full a connection as possible.

CASE STUDY

When I said at the beginning of this chapter that we've been successful because we never give our clients the booth they want to buy, I wasn't completely truthful. The fact is we do obviously listen to our clients and work closely with them so everyone's happy.

A frustrating common scenario, however, is when a client focuses more on what they want to give away at the trade show than on their actual marketing strategy, because sometimes the giveaway actually gets in the way of that all-important strategy.

For example, we had a two billion dollar company hire us to handle their exhibit at a very important trade show. As we began the planning, one of the top guys called us up and said, "We want to give away golf clubs at our booth."

First thing you should know – this company's business had nothing to do with golf. And the second thing you already know – I strongly urge clients against these kinds of irrelevant giveaways.

I said, "How do golf clubs relate to what you offer as a company?" Answer – "Well, everyone can use a good golf club." I said, "Well, golf clubs are kind of personal, people like to pick out their own." He said, "Well, they can always exchange the clubs later."

I changed the topic. "What do you want people to take away from your exhibit? What's the message?"

The executive explained that even though they were a huge company with a huge history, they had a completely new name as they were spun off from another more recognizable company. So they wanted people to remember *who they were.*

And, by the way, they were using an American Eagle prominently in their logo.

He also told me that there had been a lot of overbilling scandals in his particular industry. Their company, on the other hand, had made the billing process a lot more transparent and accountable so buyers could see exactly where their money was being spent. This was an important point of distinction between them and the competition.

All of this told me what our approach should be and how we could even make them happy with a golf club giveaway. But it had to be a special golf club giveaway that would *directly tie in* with their marketing message.

We decided to produce a company event at the trade show, separate from the exhibit. We would pre-invite those targeted customers and prospects, and get them excited about it. Our overriding message would be that this company didn't do business as usual – in other words, they weren't a part of the overbilling scandal – so the name of the event was "When par is not good enough." And then, underneath, the word "eagle' with the company's name." For those of you who don't know, "eagle" is a golf term meaning better than par or, excellence.

Yes, it was a golf event. However, our positioning for it delivered their marketing message and tied in both their logo and name.

We set up Tiger Woods video game stations where everyone could play and had putting contests and other golf-related activities. We ended up giving away two *special* golf clubs that could further amplify what we wanted to accomplish with our branding.

The first club was an "upside-down putter." A golf club usually has the bulk of its weight at the bottom, but that impacts on the accuracy of the putt. The upside-down putter, in contrast, redistributes the weight to the top of the club, improving accuracy by about a third. When the company gave this club away, they made the point that they were turning the usual process in their industry upside-down - it was not business as usual - and their accounting was going to be a lot more accurate.

The second giveaway club was a gimmicky one called the VersaClub, which you could stretch out, change the head and quickly transform it from a driver to a putter. When they handed this out to the winner, they said it symbolized the company's different capabilities and how they could quickly react to different situations.

So rather than just give out some generic clubs, we changed it up so the giveaways were special, unique items that symbolized important aspects of the brand we were trying to communicate to their prospects and customers. We took what was potentially a giveaway that would have done nothing for this company's branding and made it *all* about their branding.

THE THREE THINGS WE STRIVE FOR

There are three essential components we try to bring to the customer when we work on their trade show exhibit:

- **A GREAT ROI**

What is the return on the investment our client needs to make? If they are planning booths at several trade shows throughout the year, we break them down and create progressive targets for the various shows. That way we make sure we are meeting the goals on a per show basis with measurement and feedback so we can insure great results.

- **A GREAT ROO**

A company's exhibit isn't just about making sales during a show. It's also, as I've said earlier, about communicating the brand in an exciting, memorable way. That means we need to see what the return on our client's *objectives* was. We review how well we sold the intangibles of the company because, again, people buy later and the company wants prospects to keep them top-of-mind when that moment comes.

- **A GREAT ROC**

Finally, what was the "Return on Cool?" Everyone wants their exhibit to look amazing and "cool." It's certainly not the most important thing – let's face it, the ROI and the ROO are the reasons for a company to be at the show – but you still want to "ROC" your client's world. The "Cool" factor is something any creative company like ours *always* wants to deliver.

An effective trade show exhibit isn't a bunch of giveaways, quick sales pitches and giant company logos slapped together without a point. To really make an exhibit pay off in the ways I've enumerated, it has to be thought through just like any other marketing campaign with impact. <u>If you participate in trade shows, I urge you to go "beyond the booth" and create a memorable exhibit experience for everyone you want to impress.</u>

ABOUT RAJIV

Rajiv Kapur, president of Configurations, a company he founded in Hollywood, Florida in 1989 and which subsequently opened offices in Orlando and Tampa. Mr. Kapur has successfully positioned Configurations as a leading experiential branding, marketing, and communications firm, with its primary market in Florida. His extensive understanding of how various facets of the communications process are integrated has allowed Mr. Kapur to develop experiential branding and communications strategies for companies like Northrop Grumman, Applied Research Associates (aka ARA), Ryder Systems, Convergys, and Interval International. He received a three star Medal of Honor from the Pentagon – the highest award given to a civilian organization – for his work with the U.S. Armed Forces in designing a traveling exhibit. Configurations also designed the traveling exhibit for the Soccer Hall of Fame which displayed in Paris for the 1998 World Cup. The company has developed acquisition and retention programs designed to capture and maintain market share. Programs of this nature have been implemented for a wide variety of organizations including Office Depot, Norwegian Cruise Lines, Zimmerman and Partners, Armor Holdings, Marine Max, iAP Worldwide Services, FATS/Caswell Defense Systems, National Auto Finance/General Motors, and Ford Fusion, to name but a few. Configurations has also created a 360° Strategic Planning Program which focuses specifically on managing a company's marketing initiative as it relates to trade shows. This program was first implemented successfully for Northrop Grumman and has also been employed by customers like CHEP and Disney. This winning formula considers all stages of the marketing process, from pre-show planning to post show evaluation, and engages all levels of the marketing hierarchy from strategic planning to tactical execution.

Over the past twenty years, Mr. Kapur has established a reputation for Configurations as the prototype business after which other companies in the marketing and trade-show industries have been modeled across the country. His vision is largely responsible for successful collaboration on strategic and creative development of messaging and communications programs. Mr. Kapur has built a company that helps clients get noticed in a cluttered market by developing campaigns that extend brand experience and by designing immersive environments.

Mr. Kapur has also published articles on the hidden potential of trade shows as part of larger, integrated marketing programs. He has also lectured on the power of experiential branding. He is currently in the process of creating an educational program to tour the country, training on the latest research and developments in experiential branding. He has earned a reputation for results-oriented marketing that creates high returns on investment and opportunity. He is known for having a keen understanding of market trends and audience behavior, as well as in-depth knowledge of the issues and challenges facing emerging and growth companies. Mr. Kapur has served on the boards of the World Trade Association of Orlando and Metro Orlando International Business Council, whose efforts were devoted to increasing international trade in Central Florida, as well as having been the President of the Florida Chapter of the Exhibit Designers and Producers Association. He is a founding and current member of the American Display Alliance.